Dazzling Math Line Designs

By Cindi Mitchell

SCHOLASTIC

PROFESSIONAL BOOKS

NEW YORK • TORONTO • LONDON • AUCKLAND • SYDNEY
MEXICO CITY • NEW DELHI • HONG KONG

*To my parents, George and Dorothy Neibler, who encouraged me
to think of every problem as an opportunity.*

*To my husband, Jim Mitchell,
who has helped me turn many problems into opportunities.*

*To my children, Ben and Jeannine Mitchell,
who showed me how to teach others to do so.*

*I would like to thank my editor, Deborah Schecter, for her hard work and guidance
on this book. She has been there every step of the way to listen, encourage, and celebrate.
To borrow my students' favorite phrase, "She's awesome!"*

Cover design by Pamela Simmons
Cover photographs by Donnelly Marks
Interior design by Solutions by Design, Inc.
Interior illustrations by Cindi Mitchell

ISBN 0-590-00086-1

Contents

Introduction 5

Skills Matrix 6

Math Line Designs to Color

Tumbling Boxes (Addition: Two Digits Without Regrouping) 8

Kaleidoscope (Addition: One and Two Digits With Regrouping) 9

Blooming Octagon (Addition: Three Digits With Regrouping) 10

Super Star (Subtraction: Two Digits Without Regrouping) 11

Grandma's Quilt (Subtraction: Two Digits With Regrouping) 12

Morning Glory (Subtraction: Three Digits With Regrouping) 13

Building Blocks (Multiplication: Sixes) 14

Stargazer (Multiplication: Sevens) 15

Space Traveler (Multiplication: Sixes and Sevens) 16

Locking Boxes (Multiplication: Sevens and Eights) 17

Star-Struck Multiplication (Multiplication: Nines) 18

Exploding Star (Division: Fives) 19

Patchwork Diamonds (Division: Sevens) 20

Star Puzzle (Division: Nines) 21

Missing Blocks (Division: Mixed Practice) 22

Playing With Blocks (Division: Two Digits ÷ One Digit With No Remainder) . . 23

Fireworks (Division: Two Digits ÷ One Digit With Remainders) 24

Math Line Designs to Create

Ice Cream Cone (Addition: Two Digits Without Regrouping) 25

Bewitching Math (Addition: Two Digits With Regrouping) 26

Wave Action (Addition: One and Two Digits With Regrouping) 27

Stretching Taffy (Subtraction: One and Two Digits With Regrouping) 28

Spectacular Triangle (Multiplication: Threes) 29

Hourglass (Multiplication: Fours) 30

Rainy Day (Multiplication: Fives) 31

Spider's Web (Multiplication: Twos and Fours) 32

Sunburst (Multiplication: Threes and Fives) 33

Lacy Heart (Multiplication: Eights and Nines) 34

Power Lines (Multiplication: Mixed Practice) 35

Octagon Web (Multiplication: Two Digits x One Digit) 36

Wind Seeker (Division: Threes) 37

String Tower (Division: Twos and Threes) 38

Football (Division: Fours and Fives) 39

Over and Under (Division: Sixes and Sevens) 40

Candlelight (Division: Sevens and Eights) 41

Sparkling Diamond (Division: Two Digits ÷ One Digit With Remainders) 42

Math Line Designs to Construct

How to Make the Constructions 43

Rainbow Box (Addition: Two Digits Without Regrouping) 44

Five-Sided Pyramid (Addition: Two Digits Without Regrouping) 45

Treasure Chest (Addition: Three Addends) 46

Addition Fun (Addition: Three Digits Without Regrouping) 47

Holiday Ornament (Addition: Three Digits With Regrouping) 48

Subtraction Tepee (Subtraction: Two Digits Without Regrouping) 49

Triangles and More Triangles (Subtraction: Two Digits With Regrouping) 50

Optical Illusion (Subtraction: Two Digits With Regrouping) 51

Boxcar (Subtraction: Three Digits Without Regrouping) 52

Box of Many Colors (Subtraction: Three Digits Without Regrouping) 53

Gemstones (Subtraction: Three Digits With Regrouping) 54

Sunshine (Multiplication: Twos) 55

Triangle Twister (Multiplication: Eights) 56

Ice Crystal (Multiplication: Three Digits x One Digit) 57

Eye Dazzler (Division: Twos) 58

Leaning Cube (Division: Fours) 59

Triangle Patches (Division: Sixes) 60

Checkerboard Tent (Division: Eights) 61

Answers 62

Introduction

W hen I was teaching, my students continually begged me to give them geometric design worksheets to color. I threw up my hands, lamenting that they spent hours coloring designs but wouldn't spend 15 minutes memorizing basic math facts. It was Adam who made this brilliant remark: "Why doesn't someone make designs with math facts in them? Then you could be sure we'd learn them!" This book is for all of your students, like Adam, who are fascinated by art and geometric design and beg for more.

How to Use This Book

There are three different types of design activities in this book. Teaching tips for each type follow:

Designs to Color (pages 8–24) are geometric shapes with basic addition, subtraction, multiplication, and division problems inside them. Students solve the problems, then color the shapes based on the answers. The finished designs will make a perfect addition to your math learning center or bulletin board. For these designs, students need a basic eight-pack of crayons or colored pencils. Tell students to solve all of the problems before they start coloring.

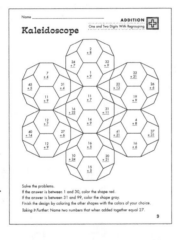

In the section **Designs to Create** (pages 25–42), students also solve addition, subtraction, multiplication, and division problems. Then they draw straight lines to connect dots beside the problems to the dots beside their answers. When all of the dots have been connected, beautiful line designs emerge that are suitable for framing. For these designs, students need a

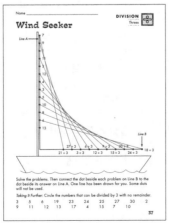

ruler, a sharp pencil, and an eraser. Again, encourage students to solve all of the problems before they start drawing. Tell them to work carefully, as many activities have more answers than problems to be solved.

Designs to Construct (pages 44–61) are fun and easy to make. Students complete addition, subtraction, multiplication, and division problems, then color the shapes based on the answers. After coloring the pattern, students simply cut it out, then fold and tape it together. (Easy assembly how-tos are provided on page 43). For these designs, students need a basic eight-pack of crayons or colored pencils, scissors, and tape. The finished products are colorful three-dimensional designs that can be hung on mobiles, used as holiday ornaments, or given as gifts.

Note: It's not necessary for second and third graders to learn the names for complex geometric shapes. But you will no doubt have some students who want to learn these technical definitions. You'll find the term for each construction listed on page 43.

To help you use this book along with your math curriculum, the chart on pages 6–7 organizes the activities by skill area and level. You can see at a glance all of the activities that focus on a specific math skill—for example, subtraction of two-digit numbers without regrouping.

Many of the activity pages include a Taking It Further problem. These problems are designed to challenge students by allowing them to apply the math operation used to complete the main design activity. Answers to these problems can be found on pages 62–64.

Don't let students stop with these activities. Invite them to create their own designs for their classmates to color, create, and construct!

Cindi Mitchell

Skills Matrix

The chart below organizes the activities in this book by skill area.

MATH SKILL	TITLE OF ACTIVITY	PAGE NUMBER
Addition: Two Digits Without Regrouping	Tumbling Boxes	8
Addition: Two Digits Without Regrouping	Ice Cream Cone	25
Addition: Two Digits Without Regrouping	Rainbow Box	44
Addition: Two Digits Without Regrouping	Five-Sided Pyramid	45
Addition: Two Digits With Regrouping	Bewitching Math	26
Addition: One and Two Digits With Regrouping	Kaleidoscope	9
Addition: One and Two Digits With Regrouping	Wave Action	27
Addition: Three Digits Without Regrouping	Addition Fun	47
Addition: Three Digits With Regrouping	Blooming Octagon	10
Addition: Three Digits With Regrouping	Holiday Ornament	48
Addition: Three Addends	Treasure Chest	46
Subtraction: Two Digits Without Regrouping	Super Star	11
Subtraction: Two Digits Without Regrouping	Subtraction Tepee	49
Subtraction: Two Digits With Regrouping	Grandma's Quilt	12
Subtraction: Two Digits With Regrouping	Triangles and More Triangles	50
Subtraction: Two Digits With Regrouping	Optical Illusion	51
Subtraction: One and Two Digits With Regrouping	Stretching Taffy	28
Subtraction: Three Digits Without Regrouping	Boxcar	52
Subtraction: Three Digits Without Regrouping	Box of Many Colors	53
Subtraction: Three Digits With Regrouping	Morning Glory	13
Subtraction: Three Digits With Regrouping	Gemstones	54
Multiplication: Twos	Sunshine	55
Multiplication: Threes	Spectacular Triangle	29
Multiplication: Fours	Hourglass	30
Multiplication: Fives	Rainy Day	31

Multiplication: Sixes	Building Blocks	14
Multiplication: Sevens	Stargazer	15
Multiplication: Eights	Triangle Twister	56
Multiplication: Nines	Star-Struck Multiplication	18
Multiplication: Twos and Fours	Spider's Web	32
Multiplication: Threes and Fives	Sunburst	33
Multiplication: Sixes and Sevens	Space Traveler	16
Multiplication: Sevens and Eights	Locking Boxes	17
Multiplication: Eights and Nines	Lacy Heart	34
Multiplication: Mixed Practice	Power Lines	35
Multiplication: Two Digits x One Digit	Octagon Web	36
Multiplication: Three Digits x One Digit	Ice Crystal	57
Division: Twos	Eye Dazzler	58
Division: Threes	Wind Seeker	37
Division: Fours	Leaning Cube	59
Division: Fives	Exploding Star	19
Division: Sixes	Triangle Patches	60
Division: Sevens	Patchwork Diamonds	20
Division: Eights	Checkerboard Tent	61
Division: Nines	Star Puzzle	21
Division: Mixed Practice	Missing Blocks	22
Division: Twos and Threes	String Tower	38
Division: Fours and Fives	Football	39
Division: Sixes and Sevens	Over and Under	40
Division: Sevens and Eights	Candlelight	41
Division: Two Digits ÷ One Digit With No Remainders	Playing With Blocks	23
Division: Two Digits ÷ One Digit With Remainders	Fireworks	24
Division: Two Digits ÷ One Digit With Remainders	Sparkling Diamond	42

Tumbling Boxes

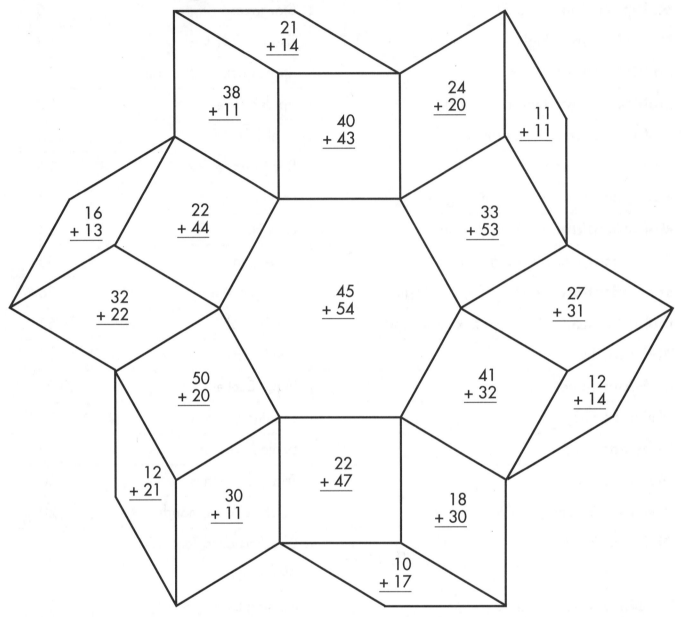

Solve the problems. Then color the design with your favorite colors. Here's how:

1. Choose four colors that you like the best.
2. Write the name of one of the colors on each line below.
3. Color the design.

If the answer is between 1 and 35, color the shape _____.

If the answer is between 36 and 60, color the shape _____.

If the answer is between 61 and 90, color the shape _____.

If the answer is between 91 and 100, color the shape _____.

Taking It Further: Order the answers on this page from largest to smallest.

Dazzling Math Line Designs Scholastic Professional Books

Kaleidoscope

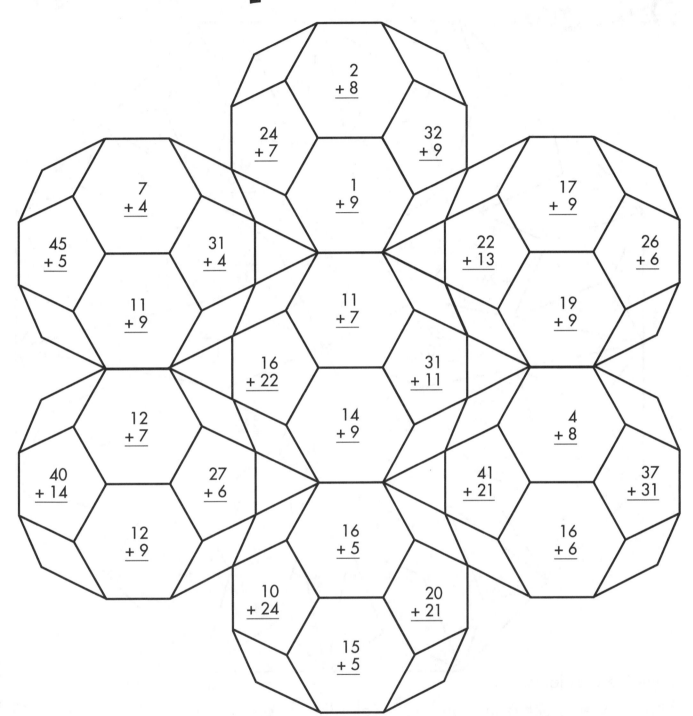

Solve the problems.

If the answer is between 1 and 30, color the shape red.

If the answer is between 31 and 99, color the shape gray.

Finish the design by coloring the other shapes with the colors of your choice.

Taking It Further: Name two numbers that when added together equal 27.

Name _____

Blooming Octagon

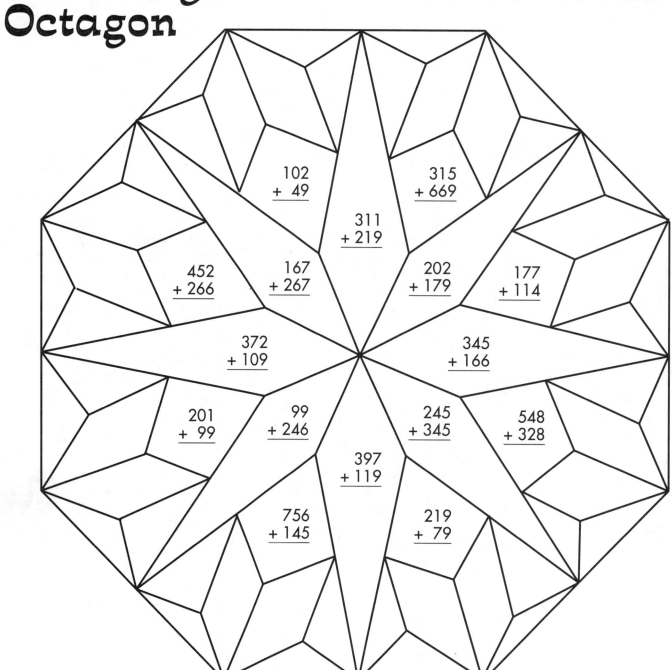

Solve the problems.

If the answer is between 1 and 300, color the shape yellow.

If the answer is between 301 and 600, color the shape green.

If the answer is between 601 and 1,000, color the shape orange.

Finish the design by coloring the outer shapes with the colors of your choice.

Taking It Further: Fill in the next three numbers in this pattern.

150, 300, 450, 600, _____, _____, _____.

Dazzling Math Line Designs Scholastic Professional Books

Super Star

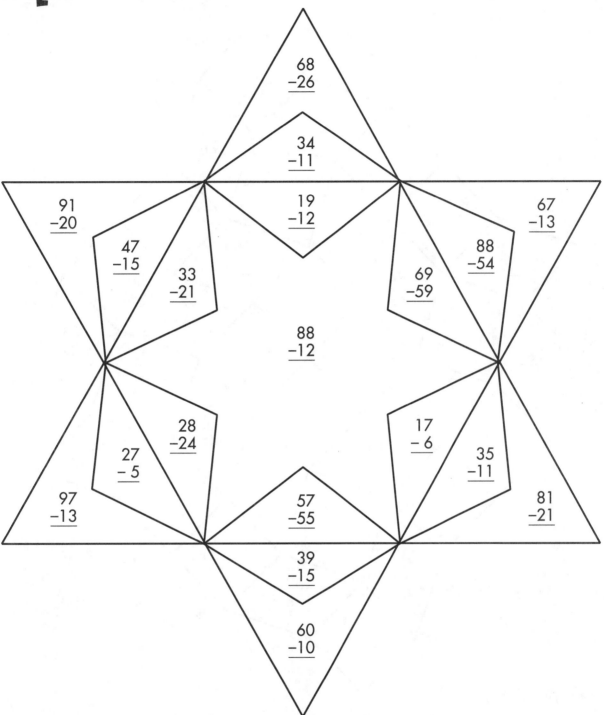

Solve the problems.

If the answer is between 1 and 20, color the shape red.

If the answer is between 21 and 40, color the shape white.

If the answer is between 41 and 90, color the shape blue.

Taking It Further: Write five subtraction problems that have answers between 10 and 20.

Name _____

Grandma's Quilt

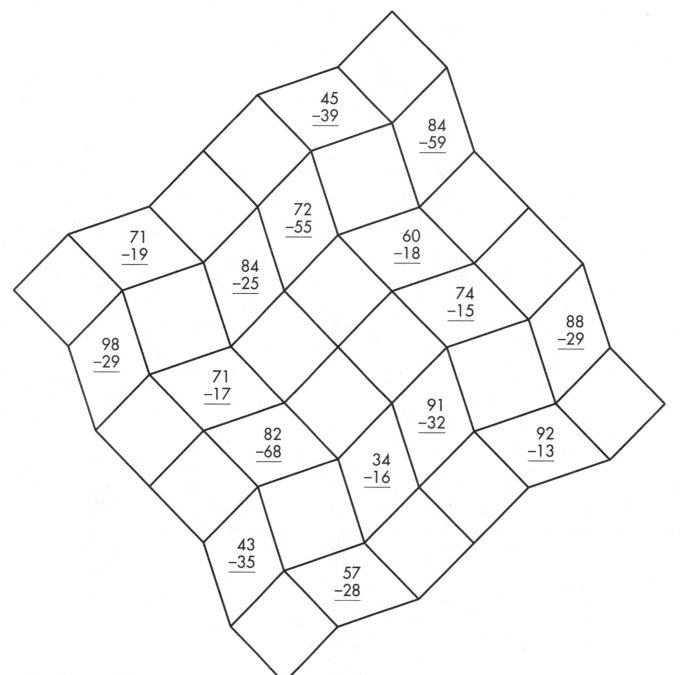

Inside the quilt shapes:

45 −39

84 −59

72 −55

60 −18

71 −19

84 −25

74 −15

88 −29

98 −29

71 −17

91 −32

92 −13

82 −68

34 −16

43 −35

57 −28

Solve the problems.

If the answer is between 1 and 50, color the shape red.

If the answer is between 51 and 100, color the shape blue.

Finish the design by coloring the other shapes with the colors of your choice.

Taking It Further: Amelia bought 30 tickets for rides at the carnival. She used 15 tickets in the first hour. How many tickets did she have left?

Dazzling Math Line Designs   Scholastic Professional Books

Morning Glory

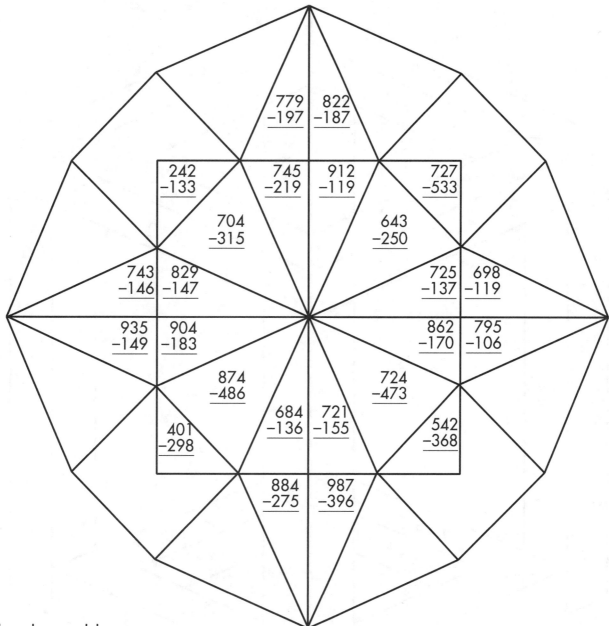

Solve the problems.

If the answer is between 0 and 250, color the shape yellow.

If the answer is between 251 and 500, color the shape purple.

If the answer is between 501 and 1,000, color the shape pink.

Finish the design by coloring the other shapes with the colors of your choice.

Taking It Further: Arrange the digits 7, 3, and 9 to make the largest number possible. Then rearrange them to make the smallest number possible. Subtract the smaller number from the larger number. Write your answer here: _____ .

Building Blocks

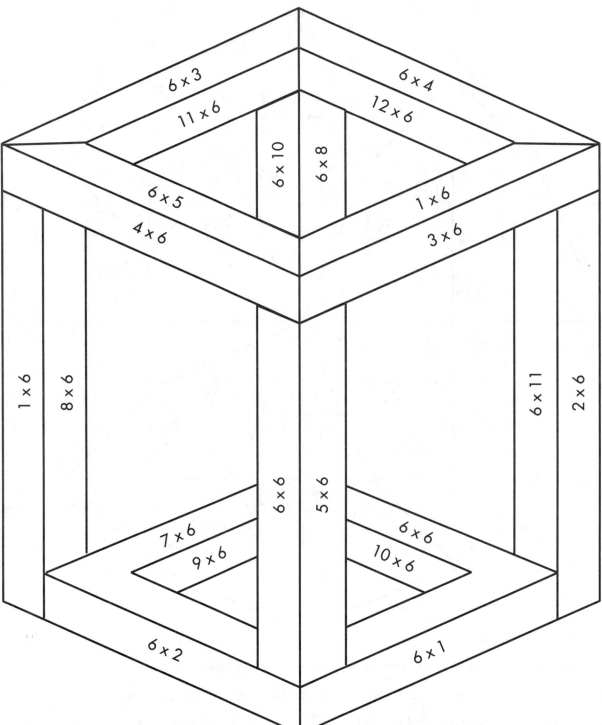

Solve the problems.

If the answer is between 1 and 42, color the shape black.

If the answer is between 43 and 72, color the shape green.

Taking It Further: Mike the mouse has 6 members in his family. How many feet are in Mike's family?

14

Dazzling Math Line Designs Scholastic Professional Books

Name _____

Stargazer

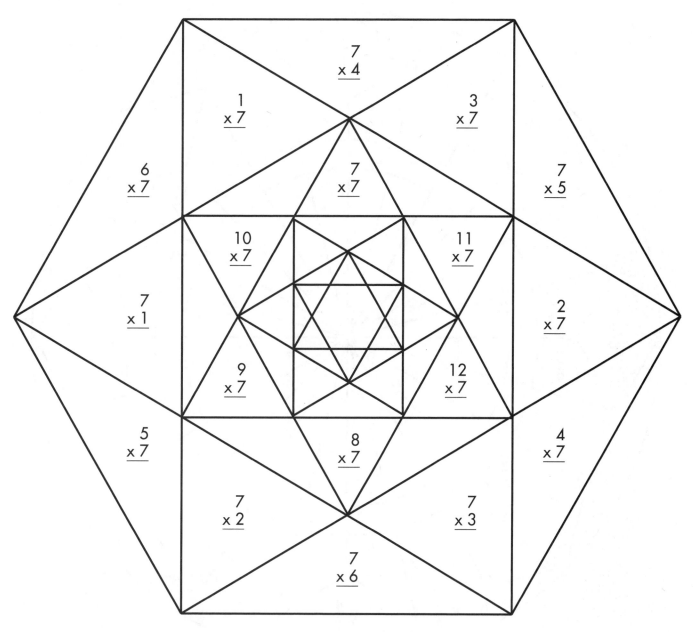

Solve the problems.

If the answer is between 1 and 21, color the shape orange.

If the answer is between 22 and 45, color the shape green.

If the answer is between 46 and 85, color the shape red.

Finish the design by coloring the other shapes with the colors of your choice.

Taking It Further: Fill in the missing numbers in this pattern.

7, 14, 21, _____, _____, 42, _____, _____, _____, 70, _____, _____.

Space Traveler

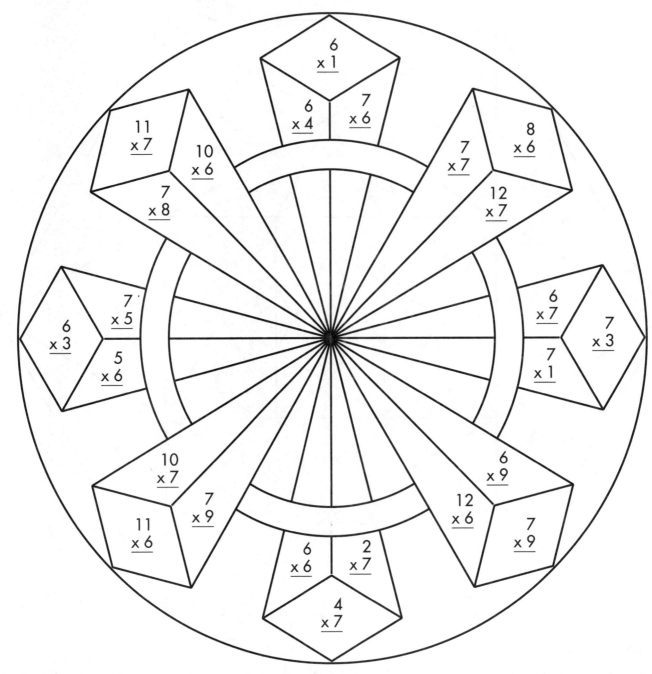

Solve the problems.

If the answer is between 0 and 45, color the shape black.

If the answer is between 46 and 85, color the shape red.

Finish the design by coloring the other shapes with the colors of your choice.

Taking It Further: Look at the four numbers below. Which two numbers, when multiplied together, are greater than 200 but less than 400?

4, 8, 23, 49

Dazzling Math Line Designs Scholastic Professional Books

Name _____

Locking Boxes

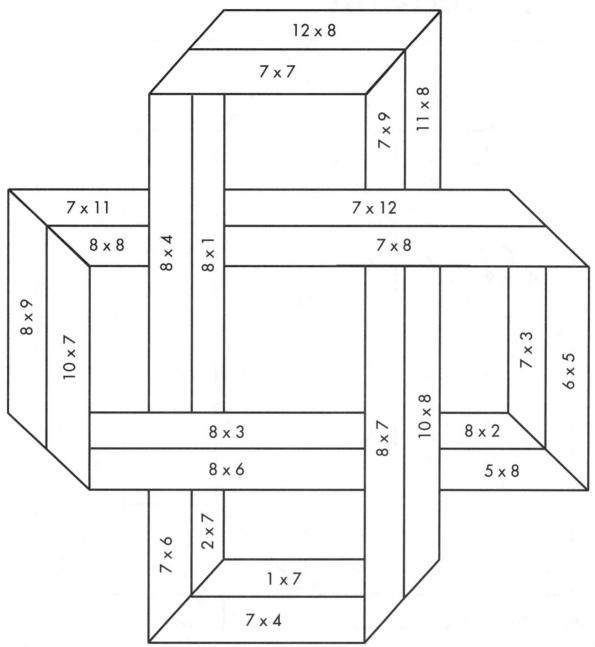

Solve the problems.

If the answer is between 0 and 24, color the shape red.

If the answer is between 25 and 48, color the shape pink.

If the answer is between 49 and 70, color the shape green.

If the answer is between 71 and 97, color the shape yellow.

Taking It Further: There are 8 people in the Chin family. If each person eats
3 cookies a day, how many days will it take the family to eat 2 dozen cookies?
(Hint: A dozen equals 12.)

Dazzling Math Line Designs   Scholastic Professional Books

Star-Struck Multiplication

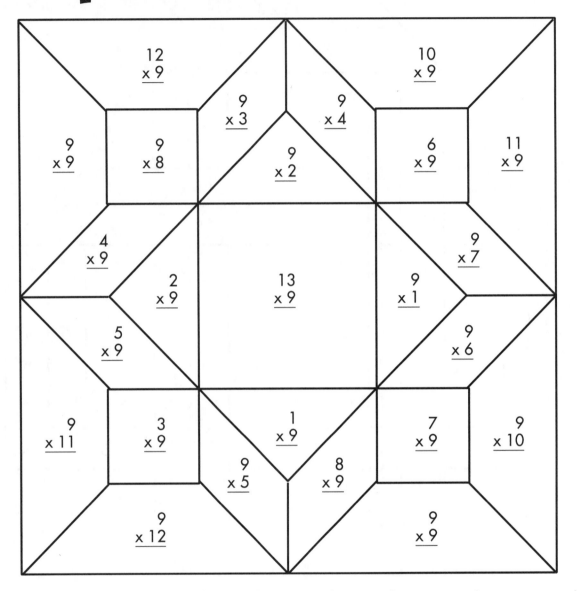

Solve the problems. Then color this design with your favorite colors. Here's how:

1. Choose three colors that you like the best.

2. Write the name of one of the colors on each line below.

3. Color the design.

If the answer is between 1 and 20, color the shape _____.

If the answer is between 21 and 75, color the shape _____.

If the answer is between 76 and 120, color the shape _____.

Taking It Further: Fill in the next three numbers in this pattern.

81, 72, 63, 54, _____, _____, _____.

18

Dazzling Math Line Designs Scholastic Professional Books

Name _____

Exploding Star

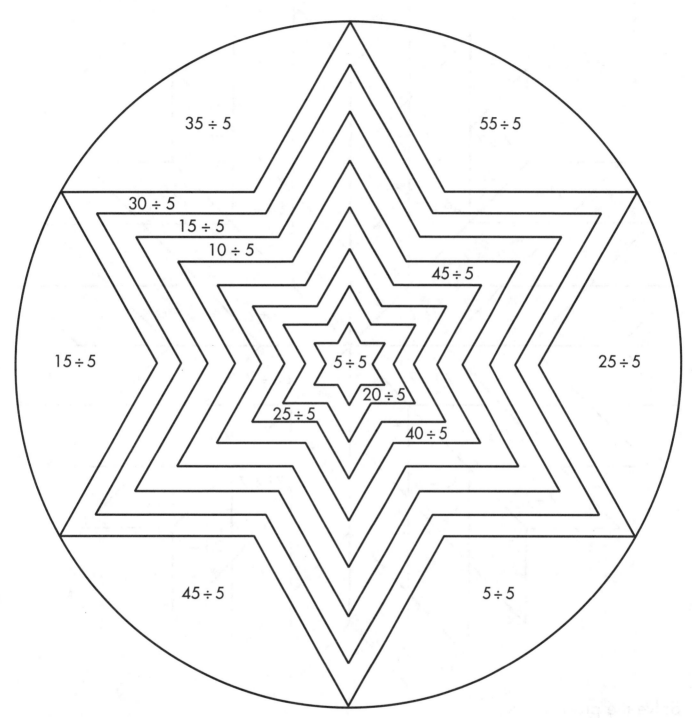

Solve the problems.

If the answer is even, color the shape blue.

If the answer is odd, color the shape orange.

Taking It Further: Circle the numbers that can be divided by 5 with no remainder.

5   8   10   15   19   20   25   30   32   33   35   40   42

Dazzling Math Line Designs   Scholastic Professional Books

Name _____

Patchwork Diamonds

Solve the problems.

If the answer is between 1 and 6, color the shape green.

If the answer is between 7 and 12, color the shape red.

Finish the design by coloring the other shapes with the colors of your choice.

Taking It Further: Jamie is making a quilt with 70 diamond-shaped pieces.
If 7 pieces make one square, how many squares will her quilt have?

Dazzling Math Line Designs Scholastic Professional Books

Star Puzzle

Dazzling Math Line Designs Scholastic Professional Books

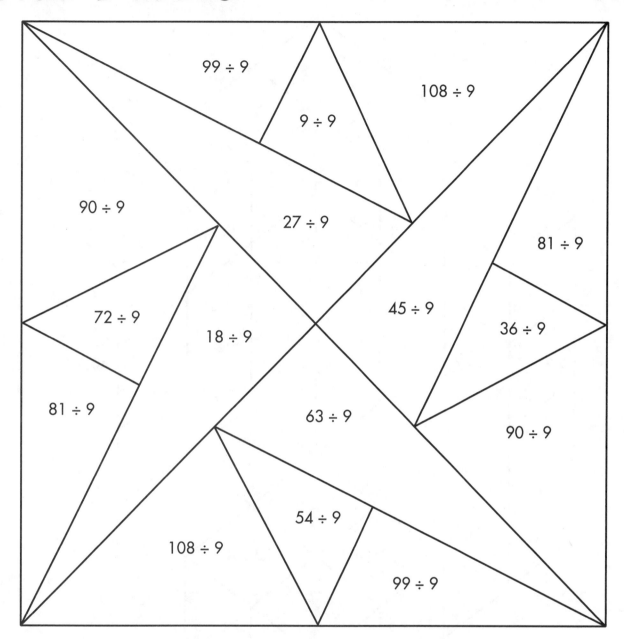

Solve the problems.

If the answer is 1 or 2, color the shape pink.

If the answer is 3 or 4, color the shape yellow.

If the answer is 5 or 6, color the shape green.

If the answer is 7 or 8, color the shape orange.

If the answer is 9, 10, 11, or 12, color the shape blue.

Taking It Further: A clerk at the grocery store took 15 bottles of soda from one box and 3 bottles of soda from another box. She put out 9 bottles of soda in each row on the shelf. How many rows were there in all?

Missing Blocks

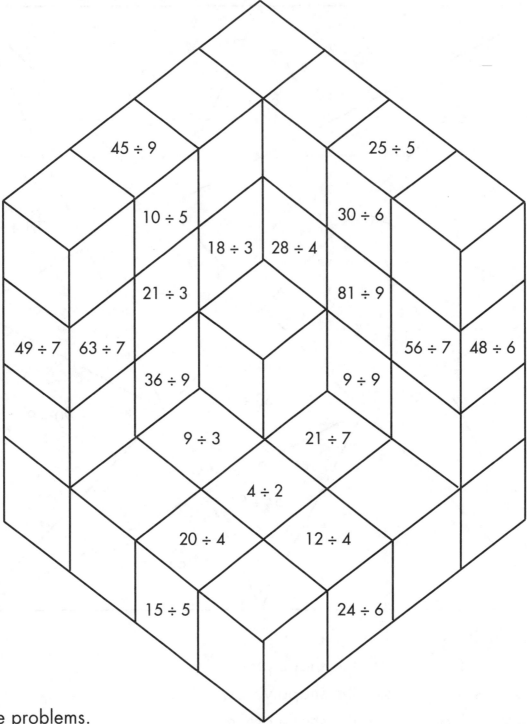

Solve the problems.

If the answer is between 1 and 5, color the shape orange.

If the answer is between 6 and 9, color the shape yellow.

Color the other shapes green.

Taking It Further: Write five different division problems that all have 7 as their answer.

Dazzling Math Line Designs Scholastic Professional Books

Playing With Blocks

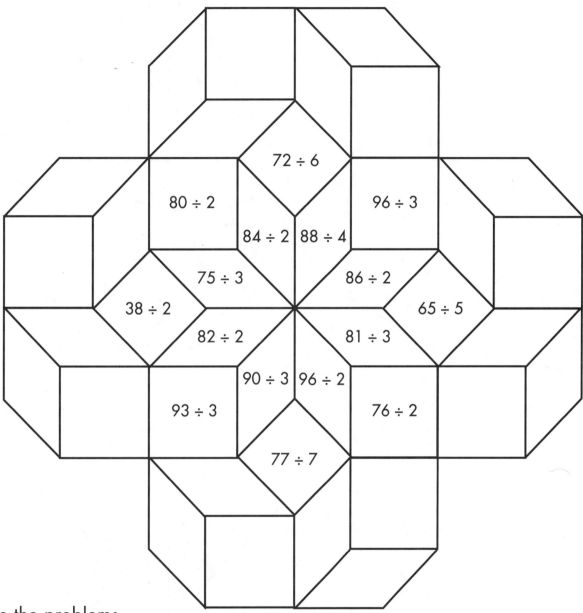

Solve the problems.

If the answer is between 1 and 20, color the shape green.

If the answer is between 21 and 30, color the shape red.

If the answer is between 31 and 40, color the shape yellow.

If the answer is between 41 and 50, color the shape pink.

Finish the design by coloring the other shapes with the colors of your choice.

Taking It Further: Tim counted 36 bird wings. If each bird had 2 wings, how many birds were there in all?

Name _____

Fireworks

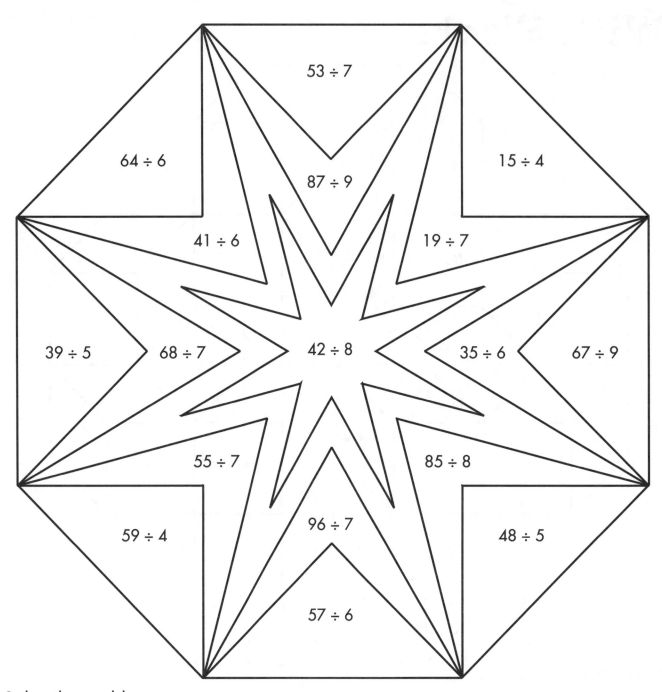

Solve the problems.

If the remainder is 1 or 2, color the shape yellow.

If the remainder is 3 or 4, color the shape red.

If the remainder is 5 or 6, color the shape orange.

Finish the design by coloring the other shapes with the colors of your choice.

Taking It Further: Rebecca had 89 pieces of candy to give to 4 friends. How many pieces did each person get? Were there any pieces left over? If so, how many?

24

Ice Cream Cone

53	62	43	64	34		46	73	32	52	53
+16	+13	+31	+24	+24		+12	+15	+42	+23	+16

Line A

69

32

64

75

71

45

47

74

85

94

62

88

25

58

Line B

Solve the problems.

Then connect the dot below each problem on Line A to the dot beside its answer on Line B. The first line has been drawn for you. Some dots on Line B will not be used.

Taking It Further: Circle the problems that have a sum of 77.

a. 42 + 35 =_____   b. 69 + 8 =_____   c. 14 + 61 =_____

d. 17 + 60 =_____   e. 13 + 64 =_____

Name _____

Bewitching Math

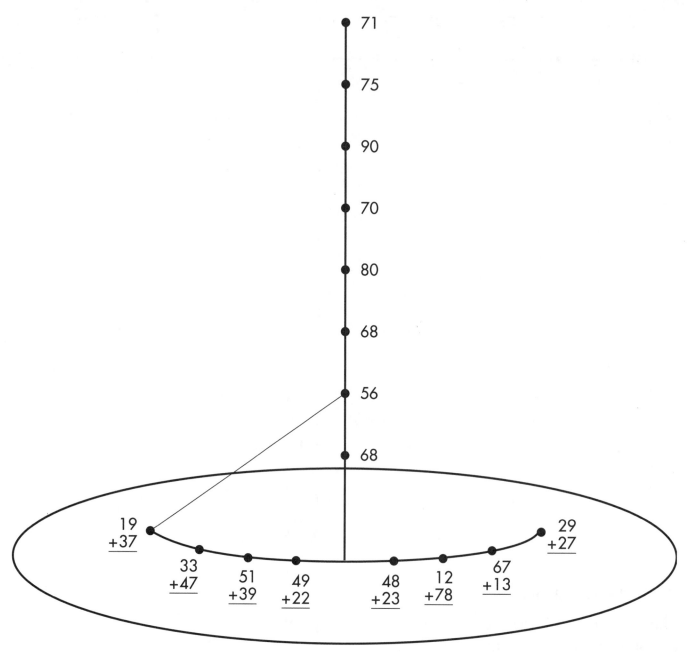

Solve the problems.

Then connect the dot above each problem to the dot beside its answer.
The first line has been drawn for you. Some dots will not be used.

Taking It Further: Fill in the missing numbers in the problems below.

```
a.  2☐        b.  5 3       c.  5 6       d.  2 8       e.  4 3       f.  4 5
  +2 7          +2☐          +1☐          +5 7          +☐7          +☐☐
  ———          ———          ———          ———          ———          ———
   5 0          8 2          7 3          ☐☐           9 0          7 1
```

Dazzling Math Line Designs Scholastic Professional Books

Name _____

Wave Action

$$\begin{array}{c}7\\+3\\\hline\end{array}\quad\begin{array}{c}16\\+14\\\hline\end{array}\quad\begin{array}{c}15\\+16\\\hline\end{array}\quad\begin{array}{c}17\\+19\\\hline\end{array}\quad\begin{array}{c}9\\+9\\\hline\end{array}\quad\begin{array}{c}5\\+8\\\hline\end{array}\quad\begin{array}{c}9\\+6\\\hline\end{array}\quad\begin{array}{c}5\\+7\\\hline\end{array}$$

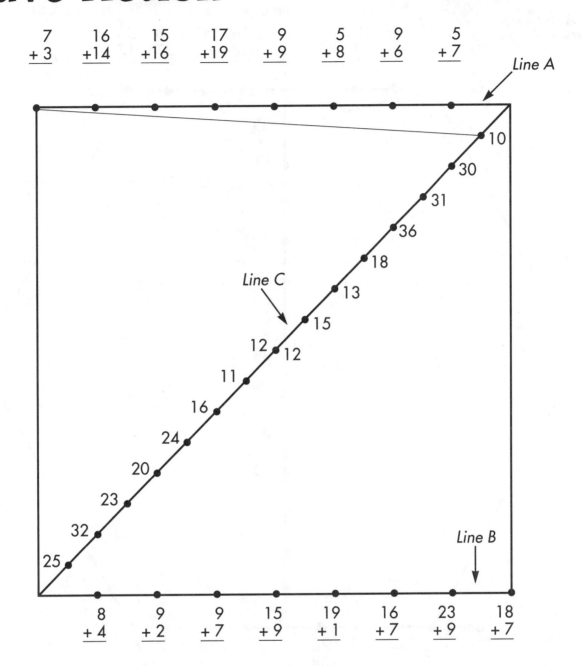

Line A

Line C

Line B

10
30
31
36
18
13
15
12
12
11
16
24
20
23
32
25

$$\begin{array}{c}8\\+4\\\hline\end{array}\quad\begin{array}{c}9\\+2\\\hline\end{array}\quad\begin{array}{c}9\\+7\\\hline\end{array}\quad\begin{array}{c}15\\+9\\\hline\end{array}\quad\begin{array}{c}19\\+1\\\hline\end{array}\quad\begin{array}{c}16\\+7\\\hline\end{array}\quad\begin{array}{c}23\\+9\\\hline\end{array}\quad\begin{array}{c}18\\+7\\\hline\end{array}$$

Solve the problems.

Then connect the dot below each problem on Line A to the dot beside its answer on Line C. The first line has been drawn for you.

Connect the dot above each problem on Line B to the dot beside its answer on Line C.

Taking It Further: Write three different addition problems that all have 11 as their answer.

Name _____

Stretching Taffy

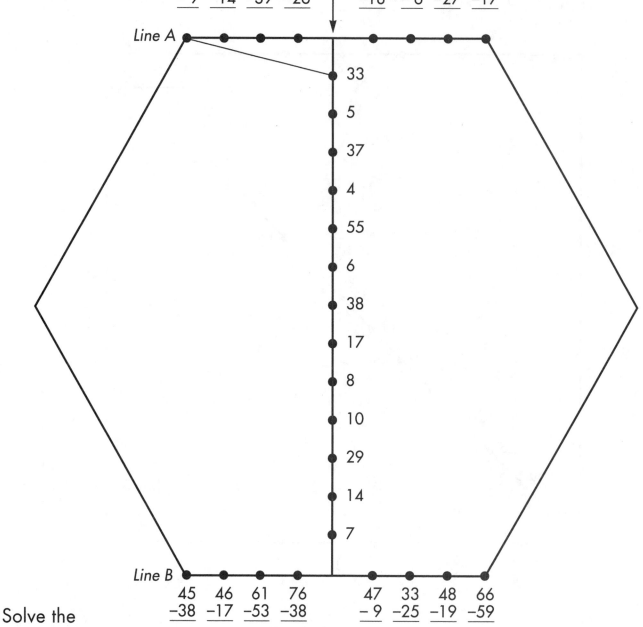

Line C

| 42 | 51 | 94 | 64 | | 56 | 61 | 64 | 50 |
| -9 | -14 | -39 | -26 | | -18 | - 6 | -27 | -17 |

Line A

33

5

37

4

55

6

38

17

8

10

29

14

7

Line B

| 45 | 46 | 61 | 76 | | 47 | 33 | 48 | 66 |
| -38 | -17 | -53 | -38 | | - 9 | -25 | -19 | -59 |

Solve the problems.

Then connect the dot below each problem on Line A to the dot beside its answer on Line C. The first line has been drawn for you.

Connect the dot above each problem on Line B to the dot beside its answer on Line C. Some dots on Line C will not be used.

Taking It Further: Amanda picked 9 flowers from her garden. She added them to some flowers in a vase. Now she has 16 flowers in all. How many flowers were in the vase to begin with?

28

Dazzling Math Line Designs Scholastic Professional Books

MULTIPLICATION

Threes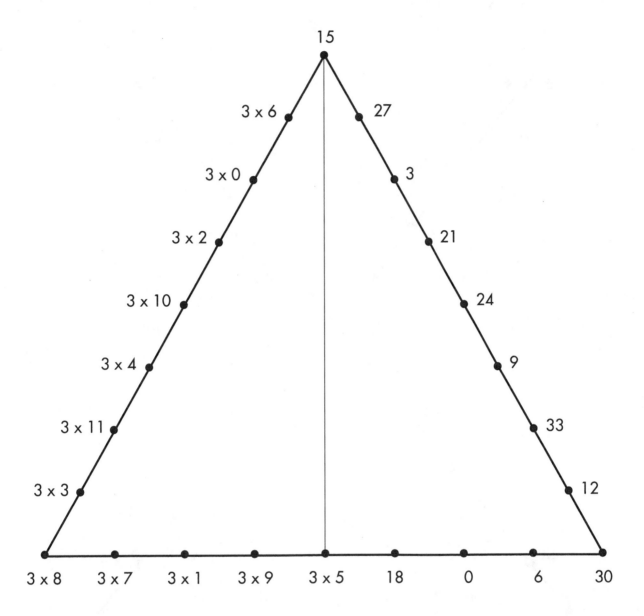

Spectacular Triangle

Solve the problems.

Then connect the dot beside each problem to the dot beside its answer.
One line has been drawn for you.

Taking It Further: Find the number that will make the equation true.

a. _____ x 7 = 21   c. 9 x _____ = 27   e. 2 x 3 = _____

b. _____ x 5 = 15   d. 3 x _____ = 24   f. 6 x 3 = _____

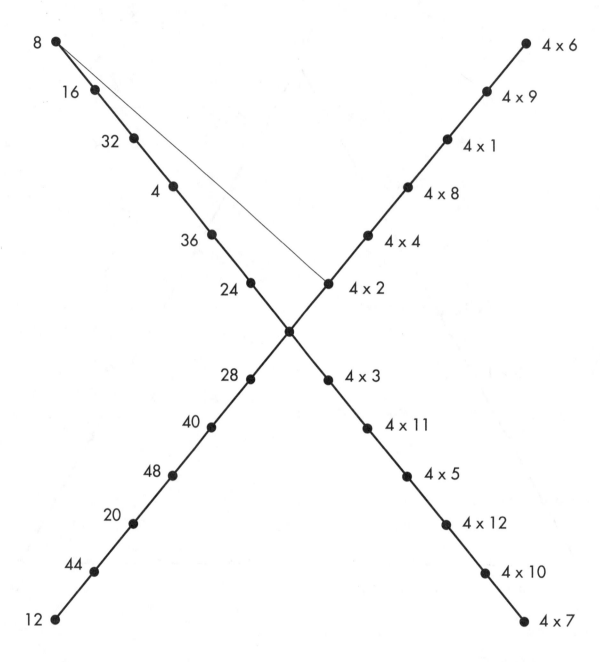

Hourglass

8

16

32

4

36

24

28

40

48

20

44

12

4 x 6

4 x 9

4 x 1

4 x 8

4 x 4

4 x 2

4 x 3

4 x 11

4 x 5

4 x 12

4 x 10

4 x 7

Solve the problems.

Then connect the dot beside each problem to the dot beside its answer.
One line has been drawn for you.

Taking It Further: Fill in the missing numbers in this pattern.

4, 8, _____, _____, 20, _____, 28, _____, 36, _____, 44, _____.

Rainy Day

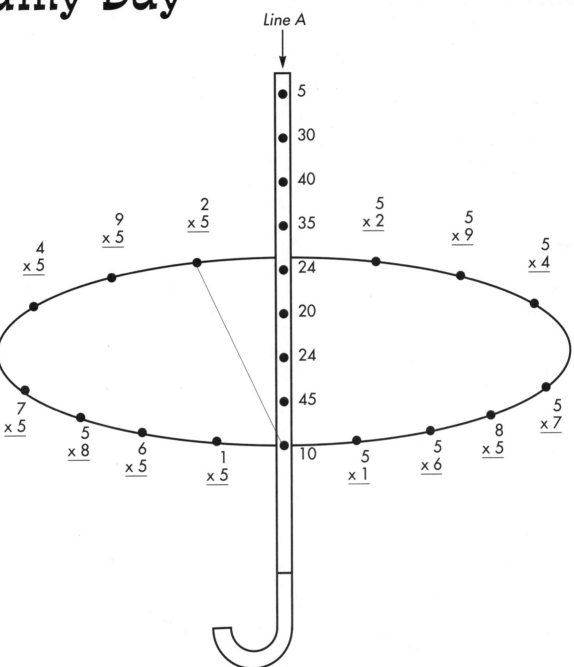

Line A

5
30
40
35
24
20
24
45
10

4 × 5
9 × 5
2 × 5
5 × 2
5 × 9
5 × 4
7 × 5
5 × 8
6 × 5
1 × 5
5 × 1
5 × 6
8 × 5
5 × 7

Solve the problems.

Then connect the dot beside each problem to the dot beside its answer on Line A. One line has been drawn for you. Some dots on Line A will not be used.

Taking It Further: Fill in the missing numbers.

a.
$$\begin{array}{r} \square\square \\ \times\ 5 \\ \hline 55 \end{array}$$

b.
$$\begin{array}{r} \square\square \\ \times\ 5 \\ \hline 50 \end{array}$$

c.
$$\begin{array}{r} 5 \\ \times\ \square \\ \hline 0 \end{array}$$

d.
$$\begin{array}{r} 5 \\ \times\ \square \\ \hline 15 \end{array}$$

e.
$$\begin{array}{r} \square \\ \times\ 5 \\ \hline 20 \end{array}$$

f.
$$\begin{array}{r} \square\square \\ \times\ 5 \\ \hline 60 \end{array}$$

Spider's Web

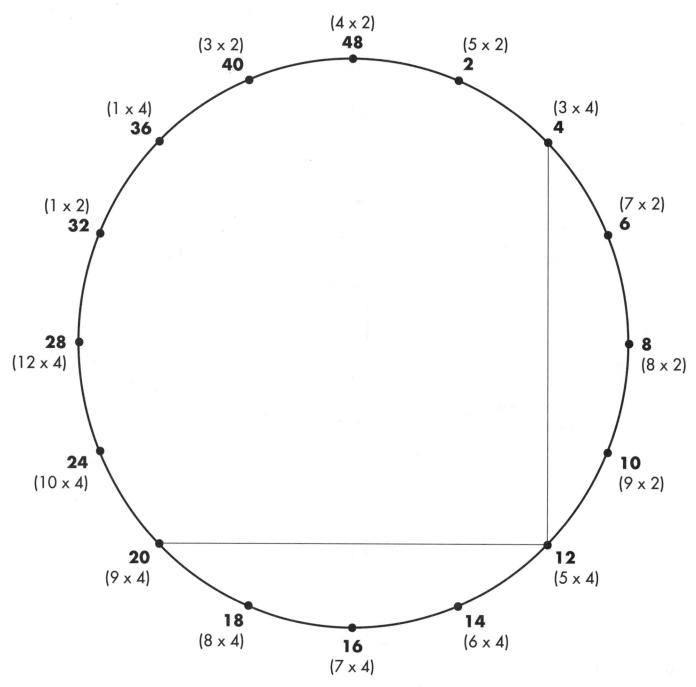

Solve the problems.

Then connect the dot beside each problem to the dot beside its answer. Two lines have been drawn for you.

Taking It Further: Nine students are making kites for science class. If they each need 3 yards of plastic, how much plastic will be needed all together?

Dazzling Math Line Designs Scholastic Professional Books

Sunburst

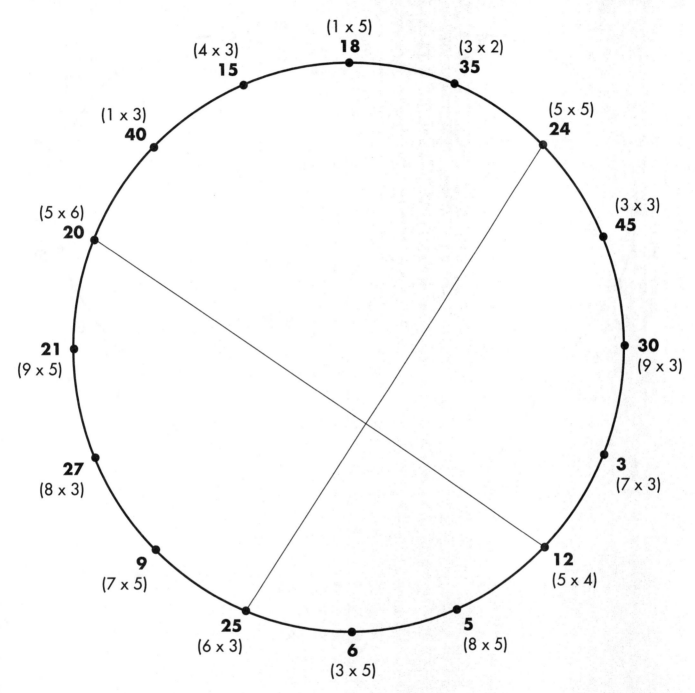

(1 x 5)
18

(4 x 3)
15

(3 x 2)
35

(1 x 3)
40

(5 x 5)
24

(5 x 6)
20

(3 x 3)
45

21
(9 x 5)

30
(9 x 3)

27
(8 x 3)

3
(7 x 3)

9
(7 x 5)

12
(5 x 4)

25
(6 x 3)

5
(8 x 5)

6
(3 x 5)

Solve the problems.

Then connect the dot beside each problem to the dot beside its answer.
Two lines have been drawn for you.

Taking It Further: Fill in the missing numbers in these two patterns.

a. 50, 45, 40, _____, _____, _____, _____, _____, _____, _____.

b. 30, 27, 24, _____, _____, _____, _____, _____, _____, _____.

Lacy Heart

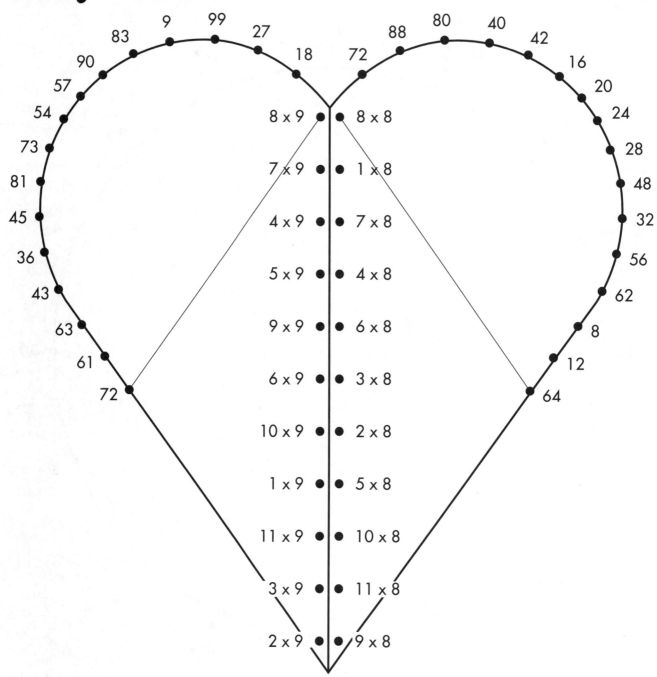

Solve the problems.

Then connect the dot beside each problem to the dot beside its answer.
Two lines have been drawn for you. Some dots will not be used.

Taking It Further: There are 81 boxes of cereal. If the clerk puts them in rows
of 9, how many rows will there be?

Dazzling Math Line Designs Scholastic Professional Books

Power Lines

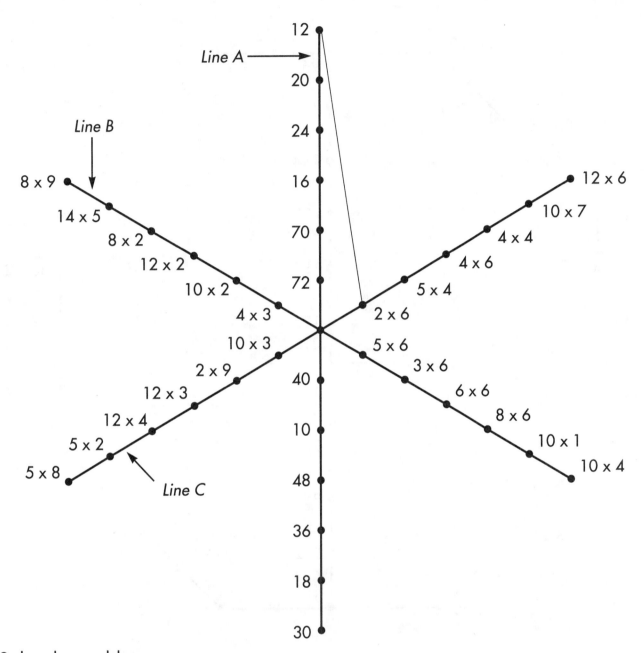

Line A →

Line B

12

20

24

16

70

72

8 x 9
14 x 5
8 x 2
12 x 2
10 x 2
4 x 3
10 x 3
2 x 9
12 x 3
12 x 4
5 x 2
5 x 8

12 x 6
10 x 7
4 x 4
4 x 6
5 x 4
2 x 6
5 x 6
3 x 6
6 x 6
8 x 6
10 x 1
10 x 4

Line C

40

10

48

36

18

30

Solve the problems.

Then connect the dot beside each problem on Lines B and C to the dot beside
its answer on Line A. One line has been drawn for you.

Taking It Further:

Fill in the missing numbers in this pattern.

12, 24, _____, 48, _____, 72, _____, _____, 108, _____, 132, _____.

Name all of the things you can think of that come in a dozen.

Name _____

Octagon Web

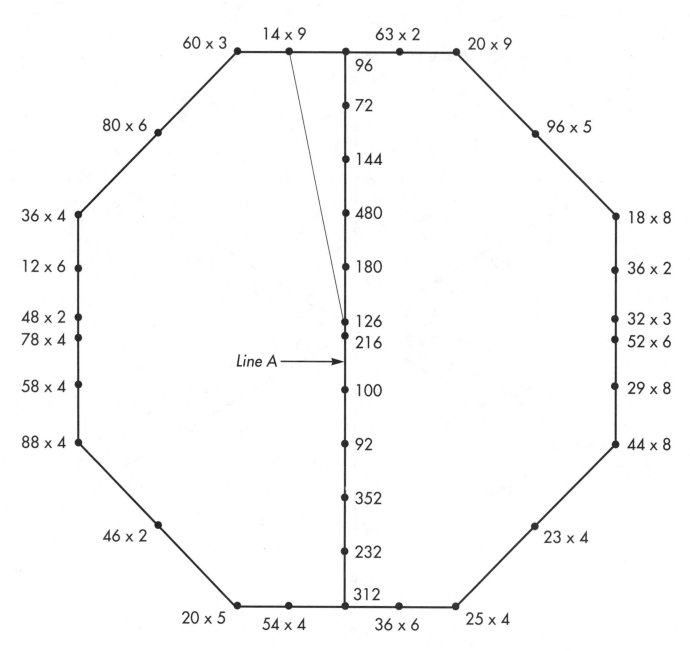

60 x 3   14 x 9   63 x 2   20 x 9

96

72

144

480

180

126

216

Line A ⟶

100

92

352

232

312

80 x 6   96 x 5

36 x 4   18 x 8

12 x 6   36 x 2

48 x 2   32 x 3
78 x 4   52 x 6

58 x 4   29 x 8

88 x 4   44 x 8

46 x 2   23 x 4

20 x 5   54 x 4   36 x 6   25 x 4

Solve the problems.

Then connect the dot beside each problem to the dot beside its answer on Line A. One line has been drawn for you.

Taking It Further: There are 27 students in class. If each student needs 4 pieces of construction paper to make an art project, how many pieces of construction paper will it take all together?

Dazzling Math Line Designs Scholastic Professional Books

Wind Seeker

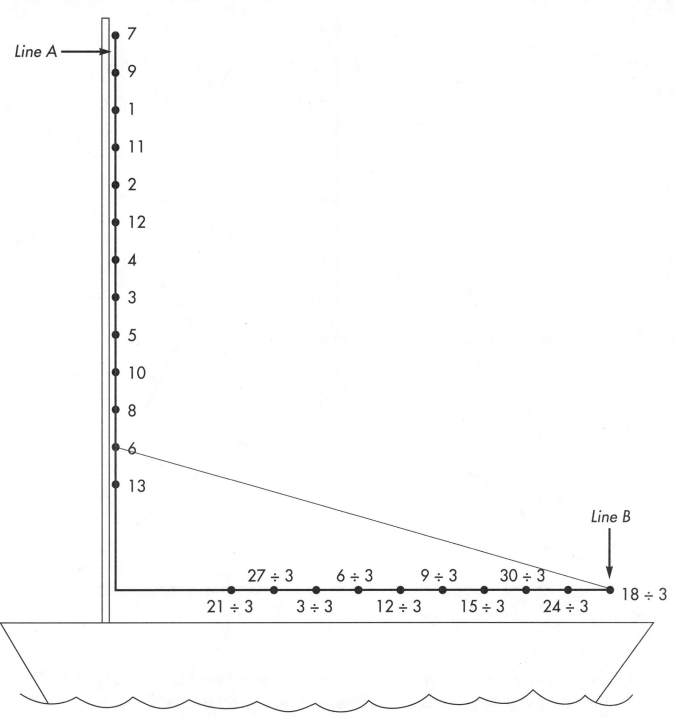

Line A →

7
9
1
11
2
12
4
3
5
10
8
6
13

Line B

27 ÷ 3   6 ÷ 3   9 ÷ 3   30 ÷ 3   18 ÷ 3

21 ÷ 3   3 ÷ 3   12 ÷ 3   15 ÷ 3   24 ÷ 3

Solve the problems. Then connect the dot beside each problem on Line B to the dot beside its answer on Line A. One line has been drawn for you. Some dots will not be used.

Taking It Further: Circle the numbers that can be divided by 3 with no remainder.

3	5	6	19	23	24	25	27	30	2
9	11	12	13	17	4	15	7	10	

Name _____

String Tower

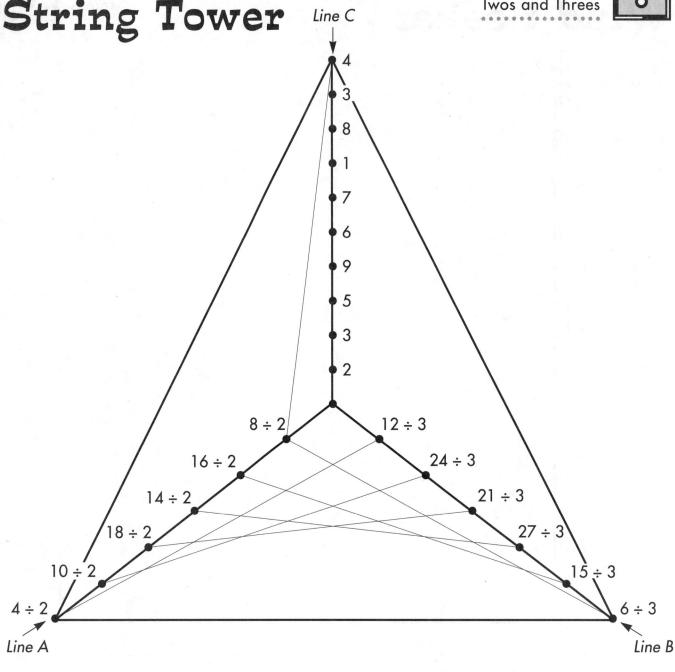

Line C

4
3
8
1
7
6
9
5
3
2

8 ÷ 2   12 ÷ 3

16 ÷ 2   24 ÷ 3

14 ÷ 2   21 ÷ 3

18 ÷ 2   27 ÷ 3

10 ÷ 2   15 ÷ 3

4 ÷ 2   6 ÷ 3

Line A   Line B

Solve the problems. Then connect the dot beside each problem on Line A with the dot beside its answer on Line C. One line has been drawn for you.

Connect the dot beside each problem on Line B to the dot beside its answer on Line C. Some dots will not be used.

Taking It Further: Solve these problems.

a. $2 \div 2 =$ _____   d. $3 \div 3 =$ _____

b. $6 \div 2 =$ _____   e. ____ $\div 3 = 3$

c. $12 \div 2 =$ _____   f. ____ $\div 3 = 6$

38

Dazzling Math Line Designs Scholastic Professional Books

Name _____

Football

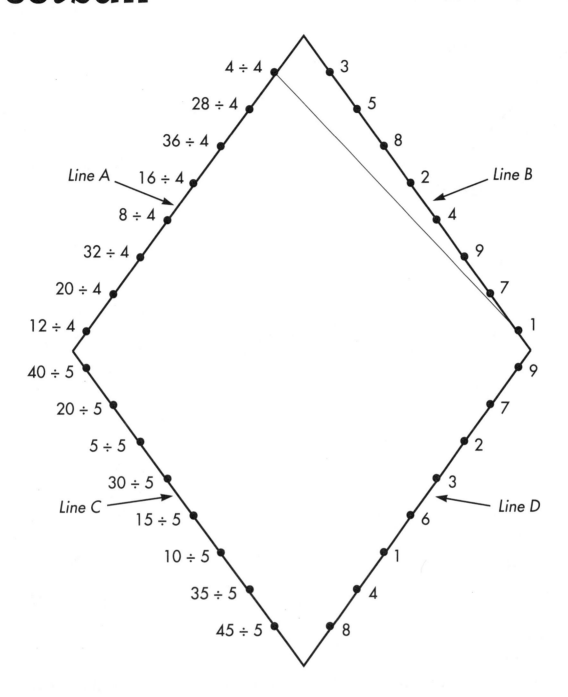

$4 \div 4$ 3

$28 \div 4$ 5

$36 \div 4$ 8

Line A $16 \div 4$ 2   Line B

$8 \div 4$ 4

$32 \div 4$ 9

$20 \div 4$ 7

$12 \div 4$ 1

$40 \div 5$ 9

$20 \div 5$ 7

$5 \div 5$ 2

$30 \div 5$ 3

Line C $15 \div 5$ 6   Line D

$10 \div 5$ 1

$35 \div 5$ 4

$45 \div 5$ 8

Solve the problems.

Then connect the dot beside each problem on Line A to the dot beside its answer on Line B. One line has been drawn for you.

Connect the dots beside each problem on Line C to the dot beside its answer on Line D.

Taking It Further: There are 40 people in line at the museum. If the guide lets them tour the museum in groups of 4, how many groups will there be?

Over and Under

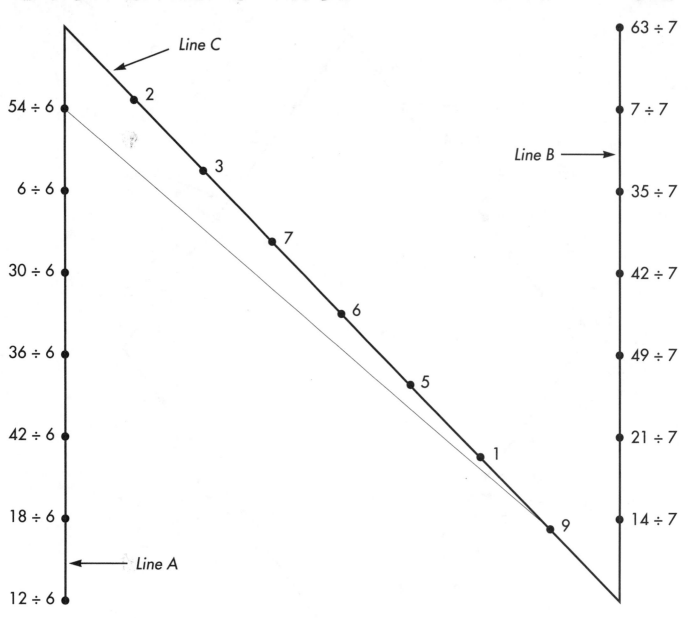

Line C

2

3

7

6

5

1

9

54 ÷ 6

6 ÷ 6

30 ÷ 6

36 ÷ 6

42 ÷ 6

18 ÷ 6

Line A

12 ÷ 6

63 ÷ 7

7 ÷ 7

Line B

35 ÷ 7

42 ÷ 7

49 ÷ 7

21 ÷ 7

14 ÷ 7

Solve the problems.

Then connect the dot beside each problem on Line A to the dot beside its answer on Line C. One line has been drawn for you.

Connect the dot beside each problem on Line B to the dot beside its answer on Line C.

Taking It Further: Solve these problems.

a. 28 ÷ 7 = ___   c. 56 ÷ 7 = ___   e. 77 ÷ 7 = ___   g. 84 ÷ 7 = ___   i. 70 ÷ 7 = ___

b. 24 ÷ 6 = ___   d. 60 ÷ 6 = ___   f. 42 ÷ 6 = ___   h. 66 ÷ 6 = ___   j. 72 ÷ 6 = ___

Dazzling Math Line Designs Scholastic Professional Books

Candlelight

Name _____

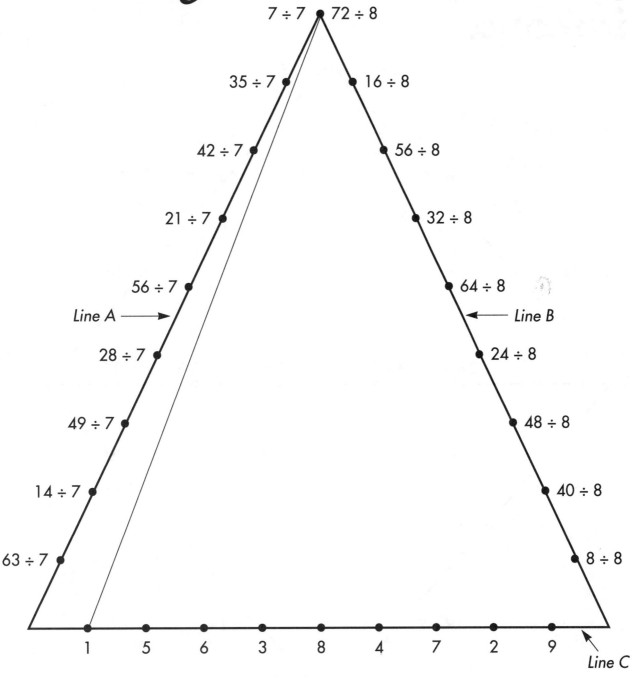

$7 \div 7$ $72 \div 8$

$35 \div 7$ $16 \div 8$

$42 \div 7$ $56 \div 8$

$21 \div 7$ $32 \div 8$

$56 \div 7$ $64 \div 8$

Line A → ← Line B

$28 \div 7$ $24 \div 8$

$49 \div 7$ $48 \div 8$

$14 \div 7$ $40 \div 8$

$63 \div 7$ $8 \div 8$

1 5 6 3 8 4 7 2 9

Line C

Solve the problems.

Then connect the dot beside each problem on Line A to the dot above its answer on Line C. One line has been drawn for you.

Connect the dot beside each problem on Line B to the dot above its answer on Line C.

Taking It Further: Write a word problem for this mathematical sentence:
$64 \div 8 = 8$.

Sparkling Diamond

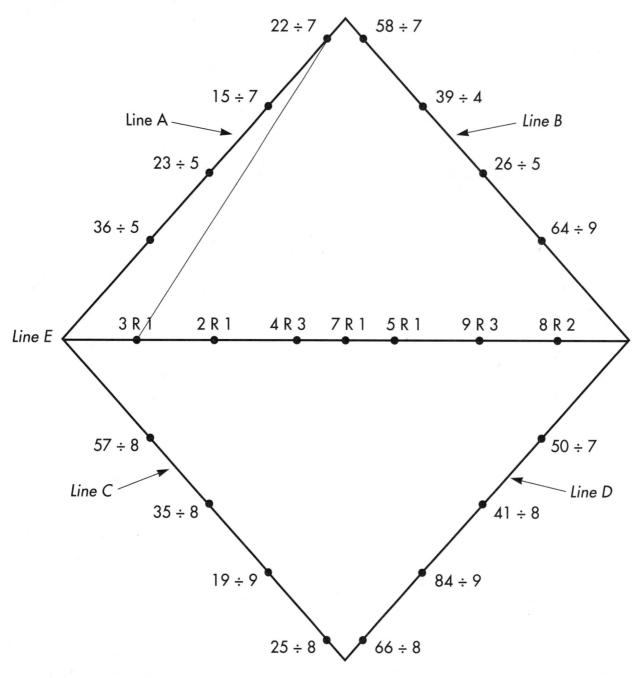

22 ÷ 7   58 ÷ 7

15 ÷ 7   39 ÷ 4

Line A   Line B

23 ÷ 5   26 ÷ 5

36 ÷ 5   64 ÷ 9

Line E   3 R 1   2 R 1   4 R 3   7 R 1   5 R 1   9 R 3   8 R 2

57 ÷ 8   50 ÷ 7

Line C   Line D

35 ÷ 8   41 ÷ 8

19 ÷ 9   84 ÷ 9

25 ÷ 8   66 ÷ 8

Solve the problems.

Then connect the dot beside each problem on Lines A, B, C, and D to the dot beside its answer on Line E. One line has been drawn for you.

Taking It Further: Five people are playing a game of cards. The entire deck of 52 cards must be divided evenly among the players. How many cards will each player get? Will there be any cards left over? If so, how many?

Dazzling Math Line Designs Scholastic Professional Books

How to Assemble the 3-D Constructions

The activity pages that follow (pages 44–61) give students the opportunity to color designs based on answers to mathematical problems and then construct them into three-dimensional shapes. While most of the designs are self-explanatory, this page gives complete construction directions.

Rainbow Box (page 44) and **Box of Many Colors** (page 53)
Cut out the pattern along the outer solid lines and fold along the dotted lines. Tape each flap to the underside of a pentagon or rectangle shape.

pentagonal prism

Five-Sided Pyramid (page 45) and **Subtraction Tepee** (page 49)
Cut out the pattern along the outer solid lines and fold along the dotted lines. Tape flap D to the underside of side D. Do the same thing with the rest of the flaps.

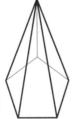
pentagonal pyramid

Treasure Chest (page 46) and **Boxcar** (page 52)
Cut out the pattern along the outer solid lines and fold along the dotted lines. Tape each flap to the underside of either a rectangle or a square shape.

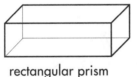
rectangular prism

Addition Fun (page 47) and **Leaning Cube** (page 59)
Cut out the pattern along the outer solid lines and fold along the dotted lines. Tape each flap to the underside of a rhombus shape.

rhombohedron

Holiday Ornament (page 48) and **Ice Crystal** (page 57)
Cut out the pattern along the outer solid lines and fold along the dotted lines. Tape each flap to the underside of a triangle shape.

octahedron

Triangles and More Triangles (page 50) and **Triangle Twister** (page 56)
Cut out the pattern along the outer solid lines and fold along the dotted lines. Tape each flap to the underside of a triangle shape.

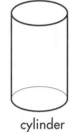
triangular pyramid

Optical Illusion (page 51) and **Gemstones** (page 54)
Cut out the pattern along the outer solid lines and fold along the dotted lines. Tape each flap to the underside of the cylinder.

cylinder

Sunshine (page 55) and **Eye Dazzler** (page 58)
Cut out the pattern along the outer solid lines and fold along the dotted lines. Tape each flap to the inside of the cone.

cone

Triangle Patches (page 60) and **Checkerboard Tent** (page 61)
Cut out the pattern along the outer solid lines and fold along the dotted lines. Tape each flap to the underside of a rectangle shape.

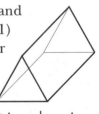
triangular prism

Rainbow Box

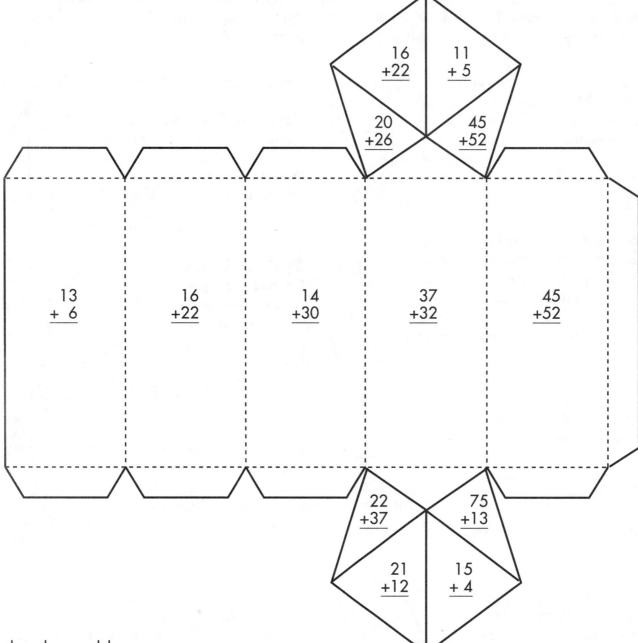

Solve the problems.

If the answer is between 1 and 20, color the shape green.

If the answer is between 21 and 40, color the shape yellow.

If the answer is between 41 and 60, color the shape orange.

If the answer is between 61 and 80, color the shape red.

If the answer is between 81 and 99,
color the shape blue.

For more fun, cut out the design and fold it into a ⬡.

44

Dazzling Math Line Designs Scholastic Professional Books

Five-Sided Pyramid

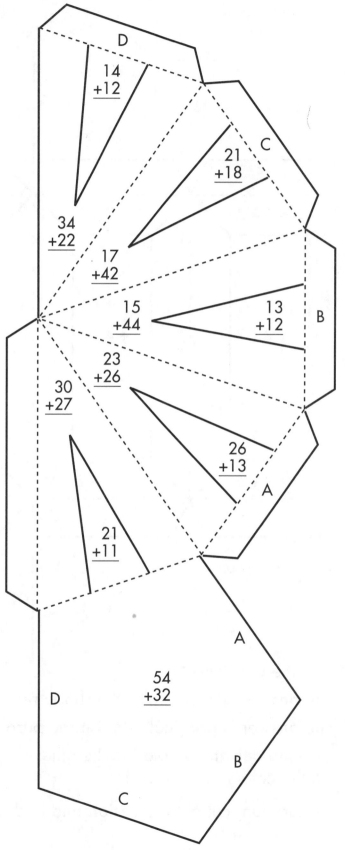

Solve the problems.

If the answer is between 1 and 40, color the shape yellow.

If the answer is between 41 and 60, color the shape green.

If the answer is between 61 and 90, color the shape orange.

For more fun, cut out the design and fold it into a .

Dazzling Math Line Designs Scholastic Professional Books

Treasure Chest

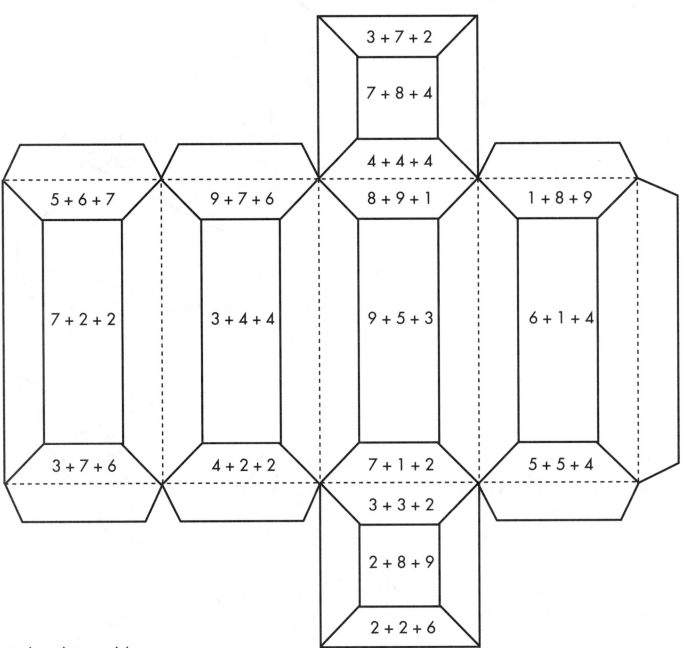

$3 + 7 + 2$

$7 + 8 + 4$

$4 + 4 + 4$

$5 + 6 + 7$ $9 + 7 + 6$ $8 + 9 + 1$ $1 + 8 + 9$

$7 + 2 + 2$ $3 + 4 + 4$ $9 + 5 + 3$ $6 + 1 + 4$

$3 + 7 + 6$ $4 + 2 + 2$ $7 + 1 + 2$ $5 + 5 + 4$

$3 + 3 + 2$

$2 + 8 + 9$

$2 + 2 + 6$

Solve the problems.

If the answer is even, color the shape red.

If the answer is odd, color the shape purple.

Finish the design by coloring the other shapes
with the colors of your choice.

For more fun, cut out the design and fold it into a .

Dazzling Math Line Designs   Scholastic Professional Books

Addition Fun

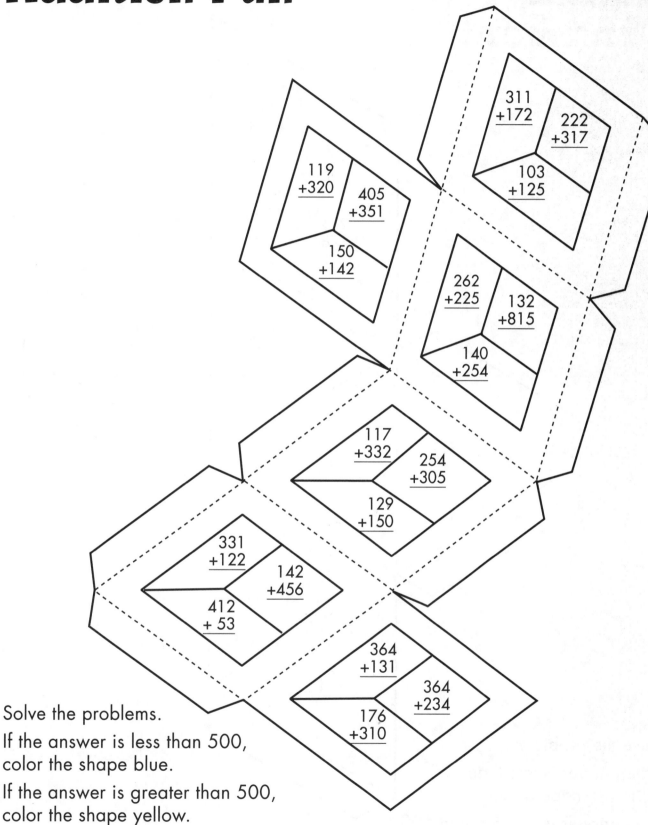

Solve the problems.

If the answer is less than 500,
color the shape blue.

If the answer is greater than 500,
color the shape yellow.

Finish the design by coloring the other shapes with the colors of your choice.

For more fun, cut out the design and fold it into a ▱.

Holiday Ornament

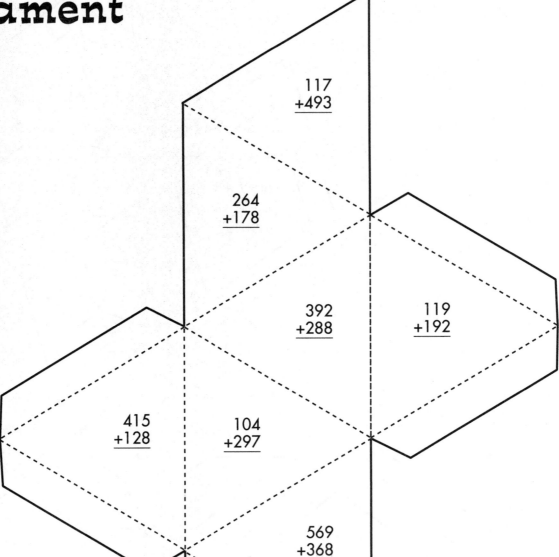

117
+493

264
+178

392
+288

119
+192

415
+128

104
+297

569
+368

199
+214

Solve the problems.

If the answer is less than 500,
color the shape green.

If the answer is greater than 500,
color the shape red.

For more fun, cut out the design and fold it into a ◇.

48

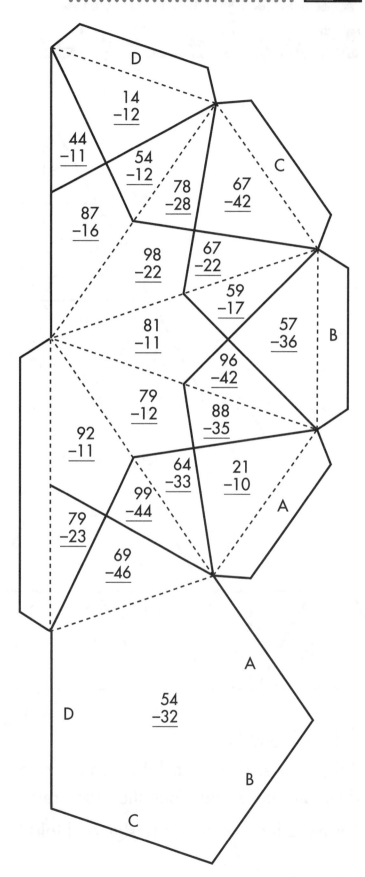

Subtraction Tepee

Solve the problems.

If the answer is between 1 and 30, color the shape blue.

If the answer is between 31 and 60, color the shape red.

If the answer is between 61 and 90, color the shape purple.

For more fun, cut out the design and fold it into a.

Triangles and More Triangles

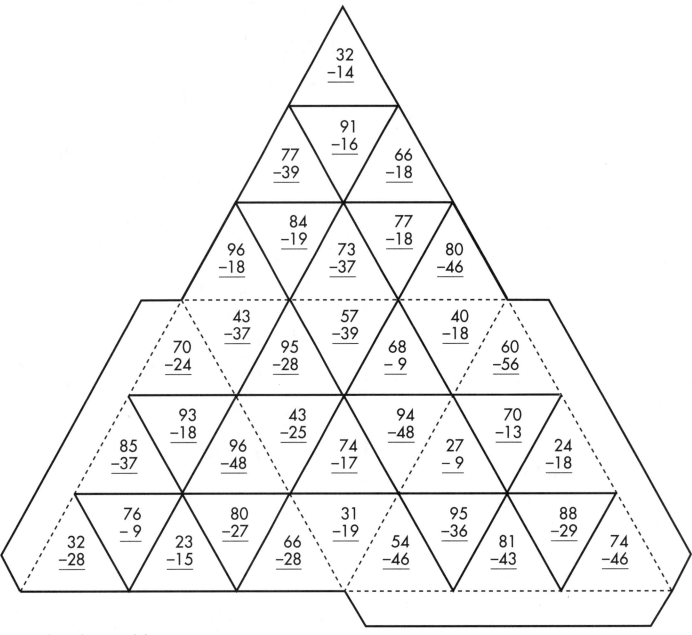

Solve the problems.

If the answer is even, color the shape blue.

If the answer is odd, color the shape red.

For more fun, cut out the design and fold it into a .

Dazzling Math Line Designs   Scholastic Professional Books

Optical Illusion

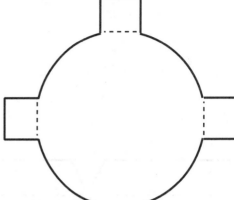

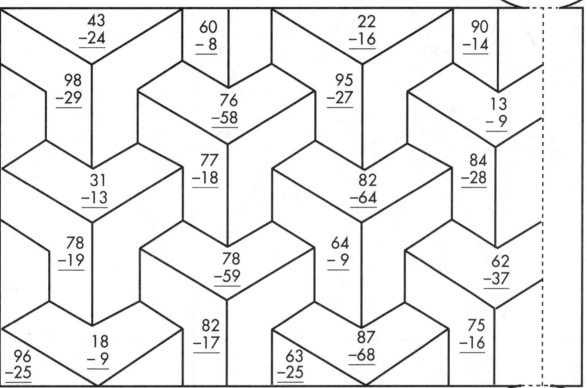

Solve the problems.

If the answer is between 0 and 25, color the shape orange.

If the answer is between 26 and 99, color the shape black.

Finish the design by coloring the other shapes with the colors of your choice.

For more fun, cut out the design and fold it into a ⬭.

Boxcar

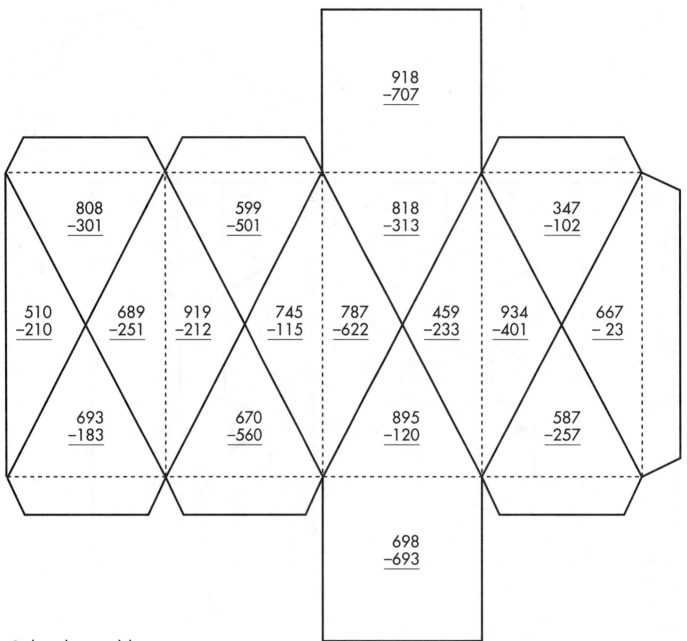

Solve the problems.

If the answer is between 1 and 500,
color the shape black.

If the answer is between 501 and 999,
color the shape red.

For more fun, cut out the design and fold it into a .

Dazzling Math Line Designs Scholastic Professional Books

Name _____

Box of Many Colors

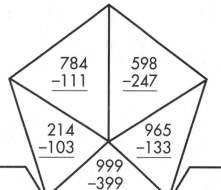

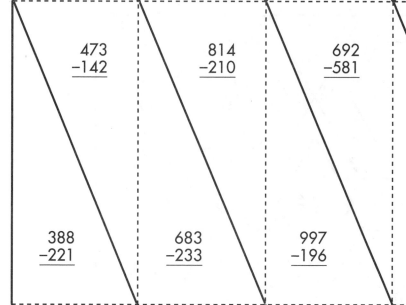

Solve the problems.

If the answer is between 0 and 200, color the shape red.

If the answer is between 201 and 400, color the shape orange.

If the answer is between 401 and 600, color the shape yellow.

If the answer is between 601 and 800, color the shape blue.

If the answer is between 801 and 999, color the shape purple.

For more fun, cut out the design and fold it into a .

Dazzling Math Line Designs Scholastic Professional Books

53

Name _____

Gemstones

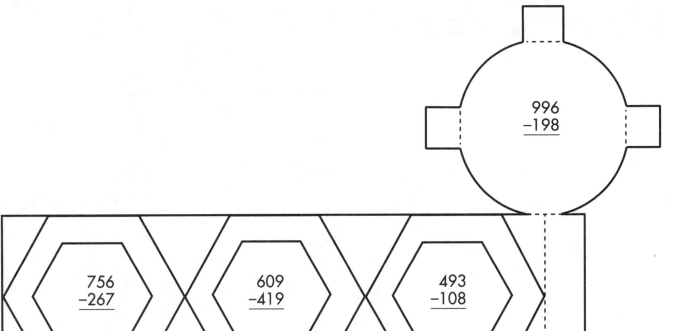

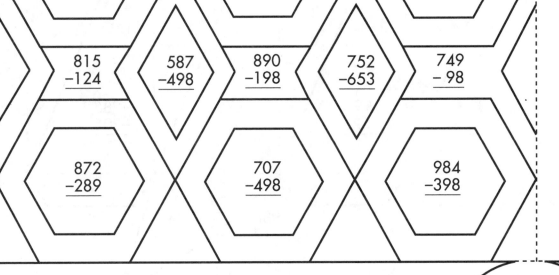

756
−267

609
−419

493
−108

815
−124

587
−498

890
−198

752
−653

749
− 98

872
−289

707
−498

984
−398

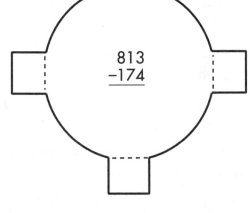

996
−198

813
−174

Solve the problems.

If the answer is between 0 and 300,
color the shape red.

If the answer is between 301 and 600,
color the shape green.

If the answer is between 601 and 999,
color the shape yellow.

Finish the design by coloring the
other shapes with the colors of your choice.

For more fun, cut out the design and fold it into a ⬭.

Dazzling Math Line Designs   Scholastic Professional Books

Sunshine

Solve the problems.

If the answer is between 1 and 12,
color the shape yellow.

If the answer is between 13 and 24,
color the shape orange.

For more fun,
cut out the design
and fold it into a △.

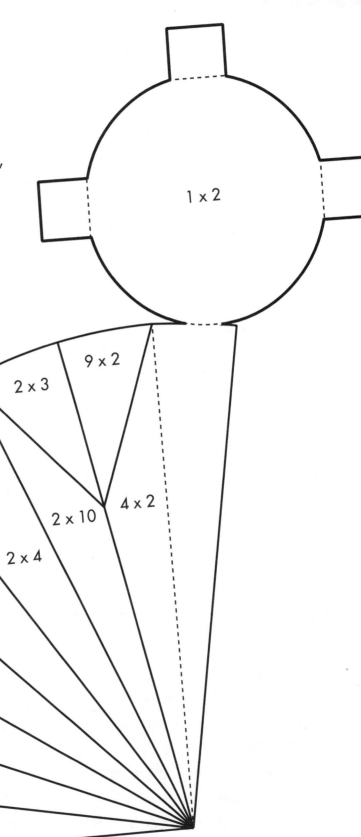

Triangle Twister

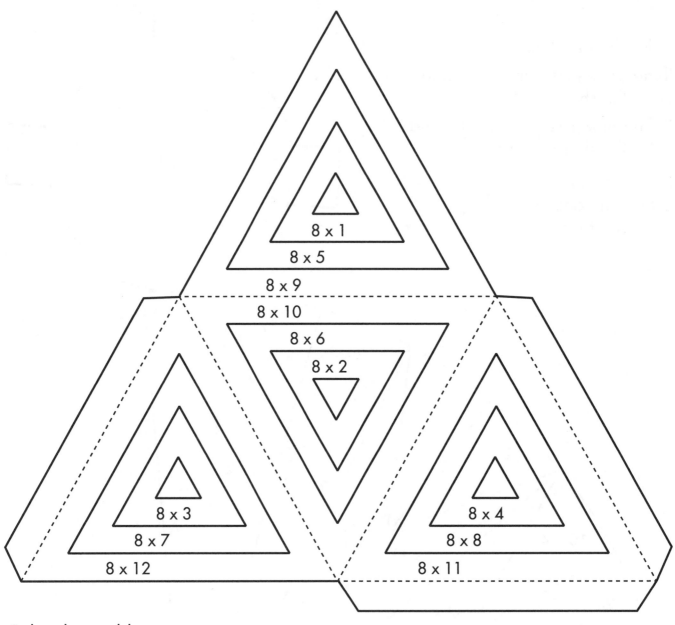

8 x 1
8 x 5
8 x 9
8 x 10
8 x 6
8 x 2
8 x 3
8 x 7
8 x 12
8 x 4
8 x 8
8 x 11

Solve the problems.

Color the center triangles yellow.

If the answer is between 1 and 33,
color the shape orange.

If the answer is between 34 and 65,
color the shape purple.

If the answer is between 66 and 99,
color the shape blue.

For more fun, cut out the design and fold it into a .

56

Ice Crystal

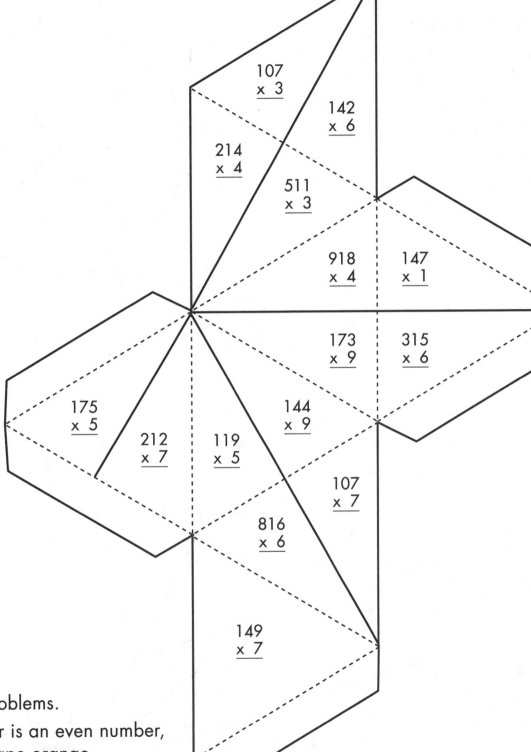

$$107 \times 3$$

$$142 \times 6$$

$$214 \times 4$$

$$511 \times 3$$

$$918 \times 4$$

$$147 \times 1$$

$$173 \times 9$$

$$315 \times 6$$

$$175 \times 5$$

$$144 \times 9$$

$$212 \times 7$$

$$119 \times 5$$

$$107 \times 7$$

$$816 \times 6$$

$$149 \times 7$$

Solve the problems.

If the answer is an even number, color the shape orange.

If the answer is an odd number, color the shape brown.

For more fun, cut out the design and fold it into a ◊.

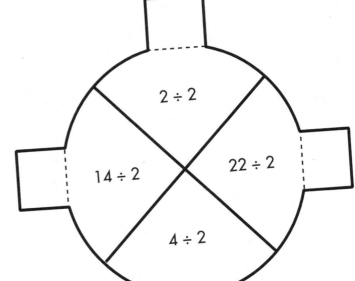

Eye Dazzler

Solve the problems.

If the answer is between 1 and 6, color the shape red.

If the answer is between 7 and 12, color the shape orange.

For more fun, cut out the design and fold it into a ◁.

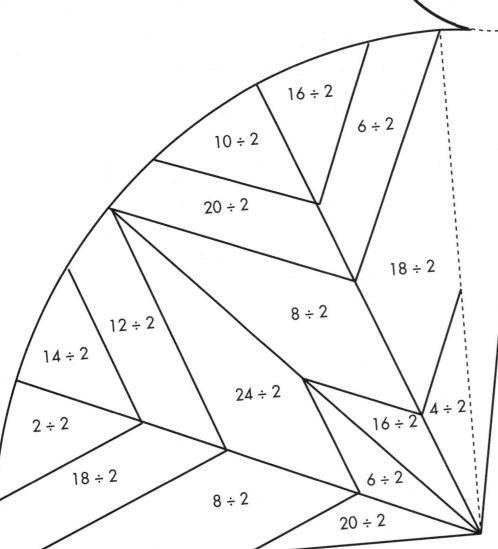

Leaning Cube

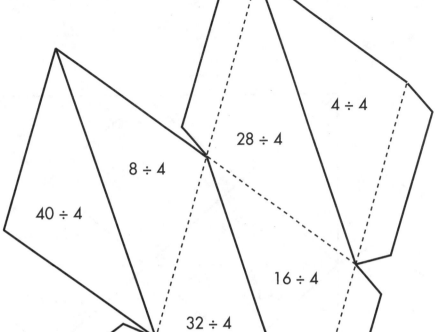

$4 \div 4$

$28 \div 4$

$8 \div 4$

$40 \div 4$

$16 \div 4$

$32 \div 4$

$12 \div 4$

$48 \div 4$

$36 \div 4$

$24 \div 4$

$44 \div 4$

$20 \div 4$

Solve the problems.

If the answer is between 1 and 6,
color the shape yellow.

If the answer is between 7 and 12,
color the shape blue.

For more fun, cut out the design and fold it into a .

Name _____

Triangle Patches

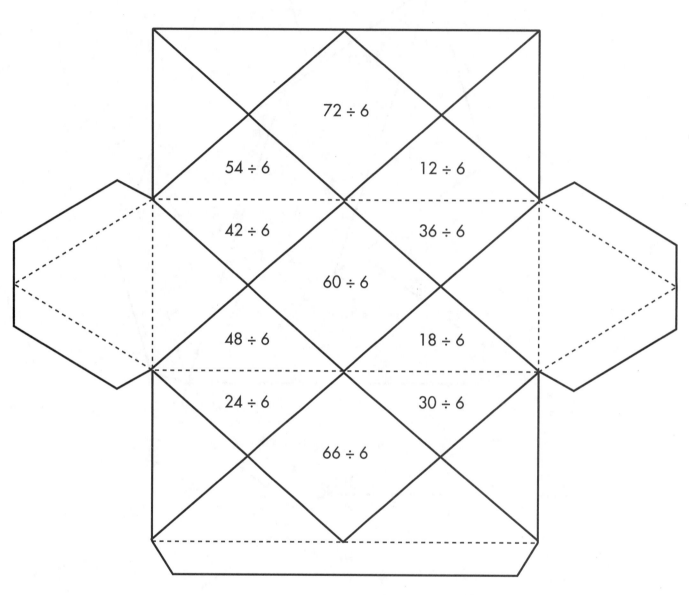

Solve the problems.

If the answer is 9 or less, color the shape green.

If the answer is 10 or greater, color the shape orange.

Finish the design by coloring the other shapes with the colors of your choice.

For more fun, cut out the design and fold it into a △.

Dazzling Math Line Designs   Scholastic Professional Books

Name _____

Checkerboard Tent

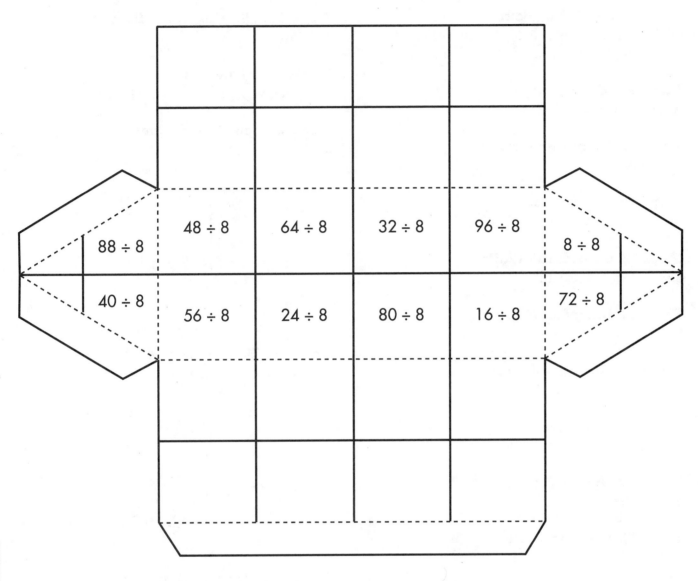

| 88 ÷ 8 | 48 ÷ 8 | 64 ÷ 8 | 32 ÷ 8 | 96 ÷ 8 | 8 ÷ 8 |
| 40 ÷ 8 | 56 ÷ 8 | 24 ÷ 8 | 80 ÷ 8 | 16 ÷ 8 | 72 ÷ 8 |

Solve the problems.

If the answer is between 1 and 6, color the shape black.

If the answer is between 7 and 12, color the shape red.

Continue the pattern by coloring
every other shape red or black.

For more fun, cut out the design and fold it into a .

Answers

Answers for *Taking It Further* questions, pages 8–42.

Page 8: Tumbling Boxes
99, 86, 83, 73, 70, 69, 66, 58, 54, 49, 48, 44, 41, 35, 33, 29, 27, 26, 22

Page 9: Kaleidoscope
Answers will vary.

Page 10: Blooming Octagon
750, 900, 1,050

Page 11: Super Star
Answers will vary.

Page 12: Grandma's Quilt
She had 15 tickets left.

Page 13: Morning Glory
594

Page 14: Building Blocks
24 feet

Page 15: Stargazer
28, 35, 49, 56, 63, 77, and 84

Page 16: Space Traveler
8 × 49 = 392

Page 17: Locking Boxes
1 day

Page 18: Star-Struck Multiplication
45, 36, and 27

Page 19: Exploding Star
5, 10, 15, 20, 25, 30, 35, 40

Page 20: Patchwork Diamonds
10 squares

Page 21: Star Puzzle
2 rows

Page 22: Missing Blocks
Answers will vary.

Page 23: Playing With Blocks
18 birds

Page 24: Fireworks
22 pieces; yes, one piece was left over.

Page 25: Ice Cream Cone
a, b, d, e

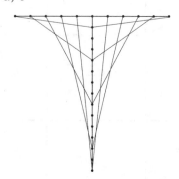

Page 26: Bewitching Math
a. 3; b. 9; c. 7; d. 85; e. 4; f. 26

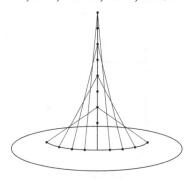

Page 27: Wave Action
Answers will vary.

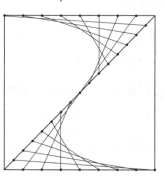

Dazzling Math Line Designs Scholastic Professional Books

Page 28: Stretching Taffy
7

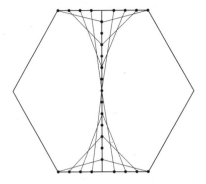

Page 29: Spectacular Triangle
a. 3; b. 3; c. 3; d. 8; e. 6; f. 18

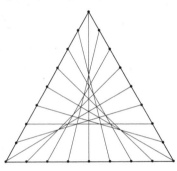

Page 30: Hourglass
Missing numbers: 12, 16, 24, 32, 40, 48

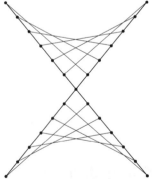

Page 31: Rainy Day
a. 11; b. 10; c. 0; d. 3; e. 4; f. 12

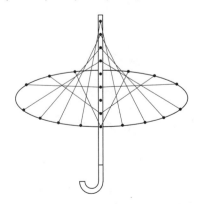

Page 32: Spider's Web
27 yards

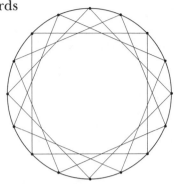

Page 33: Sunburst
a. 35, 30, 25, 20, 15, 10, 5
b. 21, 18, 15, 12, 9, 6, 3

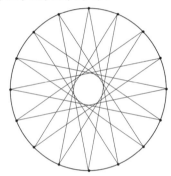

Page 34: Lacy Heart
9

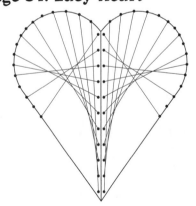

Page 35: Power Lines
Missing numbers: 36, 60, 84, 96, 120, 144;
answers will vary.

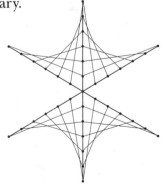

Page 36: Octagon Web
108

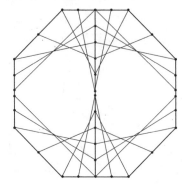

Page 37: Wind Seeker
3, 6, 24, 27, 30, 9, 12, 15

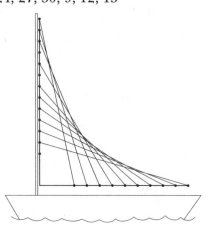

Page 38: String Tower
a. 1; b. 3; c. 6; d. 1; e. 9; f. 18

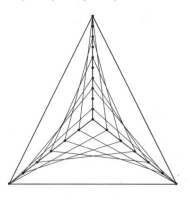

Page 39: Football
10

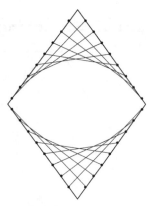

Page 40: Over and Under
a. 4; b. 4; c. 8; d. 10; e. 11; f. 7; g. 12; h. 11;
i. 10; j. 12

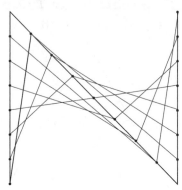

Page 41: Candlelight
Answers will vary.

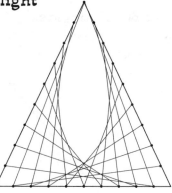

Page 42: Sparkling Diamond
10 with 2 cards left over

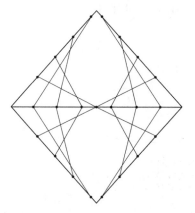

Dazzling Math Line Designs   Scholastic Professional Books